HIKING

in the

GREAT SMOKIES

by

CARSON BREWER

Price $1.00

The Holston Printing Co., Inc.
Knoxville, Tennessee

THE HIKES

I wish to thank the following who have been helpful in the preparation of this book:

Bill Dyer, a colleague at The Knoxville News-Sentinel, whose cartoons and maps will entertain you and keep you from getting lost.

Ross Bender, chief naturalist of Great Smoky Mountains National Park, who contributed invaluable assistance in a revision of the book in 1969; and Arthur Stupka, retired biologist and chief naturalist who contributed valuable information and suggestions for the original manuscript, and Neil J. Reid, another former chief naturalist who was always ready with assistance and information.

The News-Sentinel, which printed the original stories from which most of the hikes are adapted and which permitted me to use some Dyer cartoon engravings.

Carson Brewer

BEFORE YOU START HIKING

Anybody can enjoy the Great Smokies. And this book is to help you do it. It is written for laymen. While a naturalist will understand more of what he sees and hears and smells in this wild country, this doesn't mean that a banker or an electrician can't thoroughly enjoy it. You don't have to identify wood thrushes and winter wrens to thrill to their songs. Nor do you have to know that a giant tulip poplar is a member of the magnolia family to recognize it as a magnificent creation of nature.

Nowhere in Eastern America—probably nowhere in the world—exists primeval wilderness surpassing Great Smoky Mountains National Park in floral variety and natural beauty. These hikes are suggested to help you find the best of it. They are to help you enjoy it with a fullness possible only when you go into the wilderness and, for a little while, feel yourself a part of it.

Wear comfortable clothing when you hike. Comfortable shoes are particularly important. Rain is frequent and sometimes heavy in the mountains. So, unless you and the Weatherman are both certain of a fair day, carry a raincoat.

While youngsters in top physical condition may want to set speed records on the trail, it's better for most adults to set an easy pace. Rest often. You'll enjoy it more if you time your stops to look at a tree or flower or view, or to listen to a bird.

While they rarely do so, a few creatures in the Park are capable of harming a human—nearly always a foolish or careless human, though. One of these is a black bear. No matter what a friendly fellow he seems to be, he's a wild animal. He weighs up to hundreds of pounds and has sharp claws and a mouthful of teeth. Don't feed him. If you don't have enough to satisfy his appetite, it'll make him unhappy. Then he'll make you unhappy. Seeing a bear on the trail is unusual. Many stay close to campgrounds and roadside garbage cans. Those farther out in the wilderness are more fearful of people. They usually hear you and get out of your way before you see them.

Copperheads and rattlesnakes are the only poisonous snakes in the Park. Be alert for them but don't spend much time worrying about them. Don't step on a snake. Don't put your hand on one. This means you must pay some attention to the trail ahead. It means you should not cross a log without first seeing what's on the other side. Nor should you put your hand on a log or ledge without first making sure no snake is there. However, you'll see few—if any—rattlesnakes and copperheads.

Each hike story is numbered. And each hike has a matching number on the map. Mileage of each hike is given directly under the heading of each.

All right, let's go hiking!

* * * * *

Don't leave refuse of any kind—not even a candy wrapper— in the Park. Leave the Park in such condition that those who follow you will not be sorry you came.

1 THE OLD INDIAN ROAD

3½ miles, one way

See No. 1 on map

Let's suppose you want to break away for two or three hours from the cares of complex civilization. You want to walk through a green curtain into a land of 10,000 years ago, a wilderness of trees, flowers, mosses, ferns, brooks, birds and solitude.

Put on some beat-about clothing, including shoes you don't mind getting wet, and take along a sandwich or a chocolate bar. You're going to hike down the old Indian Road, from Indian Gap to the Chimneys Parking Area, on U. S. Highway 441.

Unless you don't mind retracing your steps, work out an arrangement whereby you can leave your car at the parking area, where you'll end the hike, and ride with  someone else to the starting point. To reach Indian Gap, leave U. S. 441 at Newfound Gap and drive westward about two miles on the Clingmans Dome Road.

It was at Indian Gap that the earliest road crossed the Great Smokies. Legend—maybe truthfully based, maybe not — says Indians used this trail over the mountains in the dim past. It is a fact that Confederate Col. William H. Thomas, a white man who was adopted by the Cherokees when he was a child and who later became a Cherokee chief, used Indian troops to build a passable wagon road along this route. A trail probably existed previously.

However, time and many freezes and thaws have left only a dim trail where the road existed. Faint though the trail is at some places, you can't get lost. For the trail is always within sight or sound of a tumbling stream, which goes on to join a larger stream at a point only a few yards from where your car is parked.

The trail starts at the 5272-foot level, eight feet less than a mile high. One follows it down the north (Tennessee) side of the mountain to the connection with U.S. 441 at about the 3600-foot level. The stream begins a few yards

1

down the mountain from the trail beginning. Trail and creek cross several times without benefit of foot bridges.

The stream is Road Prong of the West Fork of Little Pigeon River. Fed by numerous springs, it quickly grows larger and noisier. It jumps over falls and throws itself in foamy frolic at moss-covered boulders. It soon grows large enough to support Appalachian brook trout, lovely little fish with cherry red dots and orange bellies. They're natives, and so were all their ancestors. They were here thousands of years before the first fish ever saw the inside of a hatchery truck. This is a fish-for-fun stream; put back what you catch without injuring the fish. It's a good place to teach a youngster to use a fly rod.

Along the trail is primeval forest. All around are the sights, sounds and fragrances of nature. Everything looks nearly the same as it did when Joseph and Mary went up to Bethlehem and probably thousands of years earlier. Man's only visible mark here is the dim trail that once was a road.

A rose-breasted grosbeak, his chest colored with crimson as if his throat were cut, sits on a branch of a big yellow birch and sings the same song his ancestors sang in another birch at about the same spot thousands of years before Columbus learned to read the stars.

At one point, the trail snakes high along a hillside, overlooking the creek. Curving down the opposite hillside is something of such graceful design one might think it the work of an expert landscaper. It's a tiny stream, swiftly plunging down a curving stair-stepped bed of rock, foaming white its entire length.

A little more than a mile from the beginning of the trail is Indian Grave Flats, where one of Col. Thomas' men was buried.

A little farther downstream, you will come to an area where civilization once reached. Farmers tilled the rocky valley before it was purchased for the Park. If you search, you may find a sweet-smelling purple-fringed orchis blooming along here in June or early July.

A short time later, you'll be back to people, pavement and exhaust fumes. So don't hurry.

2 THE NATURE TRAILS
¼ mile to 1 mile, round trip
See 2-a, 2-b, etc., on map

While the longest Park trails require days to complete, some outstandingly good ones take only a few minutes to an hour. These are the 10 self-guiding nature trails, selected by Park naturalists for their interesting natural history, beauty and accessibility.

Take an information leaflet from the box at the beginning of each trail. Numbered paragraphs in the leaflet match numbered guide posts along the trails. You can drive to within a few yards of the start of each trail. All trails are irregular loops that come back to within a few feet of where they start.

The trails:

BIG LOCUST NATURE TRAIL
(2-a) Less than ¾ mile, round trip

This trail winds through a magnificent cove hardwood forest. It has one of the best wild flower displays in the mountains each spring. Part of the forest is second-growth woodland, trees 30 or more years old. However, less than a half mile from a highway traveled by millions each year, the trail will lead you into primeval forest, wilderness that has changed very little in thousands of years.

The trail entrance is off U. S. Highway 441, a few feet below the entrance to Chimneys Campground. Get a leaflet and get going. The first few yards are steep, but the grade is gentle over most of the trail.

Your first marker is at a yellow buckeye, its bark drilled by yellow-bellied sapsuckers. The second marker, a few feet from the first, is by a straight-trunked tulip poplar. Your leaflet mentions nearby piles of rocks and tells you they were piled by farmers who once tilled this soil.

This section of the Great Smokies is called the Sugarlands, because East Tennesseans years ago tapped the numerous sugar maples that grow here and made maple sugar from the sap.

3

You'll pause by trees that have claw marks of bears which stood tall on their hind legs and raked deeply into the bark with their front claws—for reasons best known only to the bears.

If you study leaflet and trees carefully, you'll learn to recognize—if you can't already—such trees as Canada hemlock, tulip poplar, basswood, buckeye, white ash, sugar maple, black birch, silverbell, yellowwood and black locust. More about the last three:

This trail was named in honor of the Park's biggest black locust, 52 inches in diameter, nearly as large as the biggest one in the world. It is at the eighth marker.

The silverbell gets its name from the delicate bell-shaped white flowers that usually open in May, about the time dogwood blooms. It's one of the prettiest trees in the mountains then.

Even within its restricted range, the yellowwood is rare. ("Knowing Your Trees," published by the American Forestry Association, says it grows naturally only in the mountains of East Tennessee and Western North Carolina, in the central sections of Tennessee and Kentucky and Northern Alabama and in a small area of Northeastern Arkansas and Southern Missouri.) However, it is common along this trail, where you can see several. It blooms in May, and the white wisteria-like flowers are beautiful. It doesn't bloom every year, though. Some years it blooms, others it doesn't, without definite pattern.

April is the best time for the small wildflowers that grow on the floor of this forest, and the second half of April usually is better than the first half. Nevertheless, you may see hepaticas leading off the wildflower parade as early as February. However, they usually restrain themselves till March.

April finds the forest floor here nearly covered with fringed phacelia, a low-growing plant with small white flowers. The phacelia makes room for several species of violets, at least three of trillium, along with spring beauties, trout lilies, Dutchman's breeches, squirrel corn, bishop's cap, wood anemone, puttyroot orchid and others.

BUCKEYE NATURE TRAIL
(2-b) ¼ mile, round trip

Except that it is less than half as long, this trail is similar to the Big Locust Trail. It has some very large buckeyes, a spectacular boulder field, and it offers a striking

4

view of the Chimneys. It loops off U. S. 441, eight miles south of Gatlinburg.

PINE-OAK NATURE TRAIL
(2-c) ¾ mile, round trip

This trail, off the Cades Cove loop road, gives you a look at a forest quite unlike what you see on the Big Locust and Buckeye Trails.

Here is a dry type forest. Pines and oaks predominate. Chestnuts once thrived here, and gaunt gray-white dead chestnut trees remain. The chestnut sprouts growing from the roots of the old dead trees will become victims of the chestnut blight before they grow very large.

Other tree species that share this forest include red maple, dogwood, several hickories and sourwood. From the tiny urn-shaped flowers of the sourwood flows nectar from which bees make the lightest-colored, best-flavored honey in the mountains. And from crooked-trunked sourwood trees East Tennessee mountaineers once made sled runners.

Bears—and humans—find huckleberries in this type forest. And if you hike this trail in late May or early June, you should find pink ladyslippers.

CADES COVE VISTA NATURE TRAIL
(2-d) Less than 1 mile, round trip

At the beginning of this trail, near the Cades Cove Campground road, you'll see how nature is reclaiming land man had cultivated during the 100 years before the area became part of the Park. You will see a branch that flows from a spring which was the refrigerator and water supply for the pioneer who built his house nearby. The spring was one of the reasons he built there.

Growing along the trail are four species of pine trees, three oaks, plus hemlock, beech, black gum, holly and striped maple. Striped maple is a small tree whose greenish bark is striped with white. It is more common in New England than in East Tennessee. Mountain laurel, flame azalea and white rhododendron grow here. The laurel and flame azalea bloom in May and early June, the rhododendron in late June or early July.

The trail gets its name from a high point that gives you a good view of the lovely, historic cove.

SPRUCE-FIR NATURE TRAIL
(2-e) ¾ mile, round trip

Walk this trail in July and August and find the coolness of May. You'll also find the flora of Canada—virgin

5

spruce and fir trees and other plants as much at home far to the North. Some of the biggest trees started growing before the American Revolution. Their roots are nourished by the moist remains of their ancestors.

Notice the rotting moss-covered logs, lying in the jumbled pattern in which they fell. High winds roaring across the mountain blew down most of these. Winter sometimes loads the trees with ice and snow, making the work of the wind easier. Also making it easier is the shallow type root system of these trees. They have no tap roots.

The trail's average altitude is about 6000 feet. Trail entrance and exit are on the Clingmans Dome road, four miles from Newfound Gap.

SMOKEMONT NATURE TRAIL
(2-f) ¾ mile, round trip

This trail, which loops off the Smokemont Campground road, is in an area that was logged until the late 1920s. So it offers a good look at natural reforestation—but not entirely natural.

Some trees you'll see are Norway spruces, not indigenous to the Great Smokies. However, the Champion Fiber Co., which owned most of the section before it became part of the Park, planted Norway spruce a few miles away, on Richland Mountain, to reforest a burned area. This probably explains the presence of these trees on this trail.

You can stand in one place on the trail and see 17 tree species.

An added attraction on this trail is that it crosses Bradley Fork Creek, a typical swift, clear mountain stream, rushing along a creekbed strewn with boulders.

MIDS BRANCH NATURE TRAIL
(2-g) 4/5 mile, round trip

This is another trail through a logged area. Most of the timber was cut 30 or 40 years ago. The land was cultivated for a time. Then it was bought for the Park. Nature is reclaiming it. First came the high "weeds" and blackberries. Pine trees generally were next to grow here. Then came hardwoods, which eventually will dominate the area suited to their growth. But pines, oaks and heath plants probably will continue to reign on the southern exposure.

The trail area is in Mids Branch Valley. The branch is a tributary to Little River. Running along the slope of one side of the valley, crossing the valley and returning along the opposite slope, the trail gives you a look at two distinct forest types.

A young cove hardwood forest grows on the relatively moist northern exposure. Tulip poplars are numerous. On the southern exposure, on the opposite side of the valley, the principal trees are pines and oaks. They don't grow as close together as the trees on the other side. There's plenty of in-between space for laurel and rhododendron. Galax, trailing arbutus and mountain tea plants are abundant.

Little River Lumber Co. logged this region. At one point on the trail is the "Y" where the logging train turned. And you can see the shallow remains of an old log slide road.

COSBY NATURE TRAIL
(2-h) ¾ mile, round trip

Entrance to this trail is near the Cosby Campground Amphitheater. It is a good wildflower trail. Notice, especially, the thick mats of partridge berry. This ground-hugging little plant extends its area by runners and suckers. It has tiny evergreen leaves. Twin flowers appear in the middle of spring, and its berries redden in autumn.

JUNGLEBROOK NATURE TRAIL
(2-i) about ¾ mile, round trip

A profusion of wild flowers, with especially good stands of large white trillium and white clintonia, makes this one of the three best nature trails for a springtime walk. The old Junglebrook log home and an old-time tub mill, powered by water from a mountain brook, offer a charming and authentic look back into the early history of mountain people. The trail loops off the Cherokee Orchard Road. It is not far from the heart of Gatlinburg.

SUGARLANDS NATURE TRAIL
(2-j) about one mile, round trip

Here is a pleasant walk in the Park for those who come to the Sugarlands Visitor Center, near Park Headquarters, and have only a little time to spend. The trail circles through mixed woodland, crosses little Fighting Creek and passes a pioneer cabin made of logs. It starts a few yards from the visitor center, at the intersection of State Highway 73 and U.S. 441.

3 NEWFOUND GAP TO INDIAN GAP
4 miles, round trip
See No. 3 on map

Winter lingers late along the crest of the Great Smokies. You'll find spring in early May as fresh and new as the cry of a new-born baby.

Park your car at Newfound Gap, and pick up the westward trail a few feet north of the Clingmans Dome Road. This is the Appalachian Trail, which meanders the mountains from Maine to Georgia, including nearly 69 miles through the highlands of the Great Smokies.

Walk about one-half mile before turning left at the first intersection. This is the Thomas Ridge Trail. Follow it through the tunnel under the Dome Road and then westward.

During the first few days of May, you should find tiny yellow violets, blue violets and bluets. Look for Dutchman's breeches on the right, just beyond the branch that tumbles down the mountain and crosses the trail.

Turn right at the next trail intersection, only a half mile from Indian Gap. This route reaches the highway a few yards east of Indian Gap. Follow the highway to the Gap, cross to the north side and pick up the Appalachian Trail again for the return to Newfound Gap.

After walking a few yards through a forest of mostly spruce and fir, you'll reach a point where the trail cuts sharply to the right. After a steep climb up and around a ridge, you'll be out of the spruce and fir and into a sparse forest of deciduous trees, largely stunted beech and birch.

Before beech and birch leaves come out, the ground under the trees is covered with spring beauties. Acres of these tiny plants have masses of white and pale pink bloom. It's one of the prettiest sights in the Park.

Trout lilies bloom at the same time or a few days earlier. White trillium often is just popping out of the ground when the spring beauties are at their best. These mountain-top trillium are much smaller than the same species that grow in the coves 2000 to 4000 feet lower.

8

While spring is the most pleasant time to make this hike, it is good any time—except when it is under several inches of snow. It's a good hot-weather hike because it's never hot up here. All of the trail is more than 5000 feet above sea level.

One spring-blooming shrub on the trail is hobble bush, spindly and awkward looking as an adolescent boy. It sprouts wrinkly leaves, round and faintly heartshaped, growing opposite each other. Between the leaves are clusters of white blossoms. In autumn, the leaves are among the first in the forest to change color. They turn every shade from waxy, orange-red to dark wine. The bushes have bright red berries in fall.

* * * * * *

Bears ride down sourwood saplings to get Sphinx moth larva which eat sourwood leaves.

* * * * * *

It's a good idea to carry an extra pair of socks on a long hike.

4 SPENCE FIELD AND THUNDERHEAD
14.4 miles, round trip
See No. 4 on map

Some hike to find solitude in still forests. Others look for natural beauty. A few want to match their muscles and stamina against these long trails to the highlands.

This jaunt to Spence Field and Thunderhead fills all these purposes.

The trail starts at the upper end of the Cades Cove picnic area. For about two miles, it stays close to Anthony Creek, a small stream that sings along between flower-bordered banks. Anthony Creek Valley has some big tulip poplars, hemlocks, basswoods and other cove hardwood trees. Look for a particularly large hemlock, to the right of the trail, about one-half mile beyond the one-log foot bridge. Then, on the left side, a half mile farther, notice a large hemlock whose root system is arched like a foot over a big rock.

It's a good trail for wild flowers. Trillium is outstanding and comes in at least six different species. Prettiest is painted trillium. Its three petals are mostly white but are tinted rose-pink near the base. This trillium grows only at fairly high elevations. You'll see it first on this trail 3800 to 4000 feet above sea level.

Spence Field is the largest grass bald in the Great Smokies. It has roughly 30 acres of thick wild grass. Sheep and cattle grazed on it before it became part of the Park. The springy grass makes a restful mattress for a tired hiker.

The bald has a scattering of serviceberry trees, but you may not recognize them if you're accustomed to seeing them in woodland. These on the bald are different—sturdy, thickly branched and not nearly as tall as those growing in the woods. These probably developed their peculiar characteristics to withstand the fierce winds that sometimes lash the mountaintop. While lowland serviceberry trees usually bloom in March or early April, these on Spence Field bloom about a month later. Spring comes that much later at this 4958-foot altitude.

I can't say exactly where Spence Field ends and Thunderhead Mountain begins. But two miles and four peaks — with deep saddles between them — separate the Spence Field and Thunderhead markers.

Thunderhead is 5527 feet above sea level. So the net altitude gain over Spence Field is only 569 feet. However, you climb nearly three times that much, only to lose most of it in the saddles between the peaks. While Spence Field is a grass bald, the top of Thunderhead is a heath bald. A few struggling trees grow at some points between the two.

One of the peaks between Spence Field and Thunderhead is called Rocky Top. When you see the jumble of broken gray rocks, you'll understand why.

Views from the peaks are worth the climb. Down south are pieces of Fontana Lake, like jigsaw puzzle pieces of a jade dragon. A finger of lake arrowing back toward you is Eagle Creek embayment. Lakes to be seen in the distance include Chilhowee, Douglas and maybe Fort Loudoun.

Then, there are good views of Cades Cove's emerald meadows.

Stretching down and away on all sides are the mountains, clothed in dark green of hemlock and pine and lighter green of deciduous forest. Clouds constantly change the light pattern on the hills.

Rest while you look, and the trail back will be easier.

If you feel the round trip is too much for one day, carry blankets and extra food and spend the night at the Appalachian Trail shelter. Cold water flows from a nearby spring.

* * * * * *

Spring wildflowers normally reach their best in the Great Smokies toward the end of April. A Spring Wildflower Pilgrimage is held each year on Thursday, Friday and Saturday of the last weekend of April.

11

5 ABRAMS FALLS
5 miles, round trip
See No. 5 on map

Abrams Creek plunges over Abrams Falls into the largest natural pool in the Park. Flecked with dancing bubbles of foam, deep and cold and bordered with ledges of gray rock, it is a fishing hole, swimming hole and a lovely place to see.

A huge rock ledge on one side is just the right height for a fishing platform.

Abrams Creek is the largest stream entirely inside the park. It drains an area considered by many to be the most beautiful in the Park — Cades Cove and the mountains around it.

The stream has dozens of tributaries and their names range the alphabet from Anthony Creek to Wildcat Branch. Many tumble clear and cold and boisterous down the mountainside into the Cove. There they slow their pace, join the main stream and meander quietly through the flat-to-gently-rolling Cove. Fat cattle and deer drink from the creek.

On its trip through the Cove, Abrams Creek encounters limestone, uncommon in the Park. Many trout fishermen think Abrams Creek, below the Cove, is the best fishing stream in the Park. Some ichthyologists say the limestone factor is the reason trout grow a little larger there, on the average, than those in other Park streams. They say limestone provides a better habitat for the small creatures trout eat.

John Oliver, the great-grandson of the John Oliver who was the first settler in Cades Cove, planted 10,000 rainbow fingerlings in the creek in 1908. These were the first rainbow planted in waters now inside the Park. Previously, brook trout were the only trout in the Smokies streams.

Brookies now live in the small streams in the high elevations, while rainbows are the most sought fish in lower streams.

Hikers who also happen to be trout fishermen may want to take part of this hike in the creek. But a word of warning: Abrams Creek has the slipperiest bottom of any stream in the mountains. And a fisherman must stay in the creek most of the way, for the banks are so thickly covered with laurel, rhododendron and trees that casting from them is very difficult.

To reach the creek and the start of the trail, follow the one-way loop road half way around the Cove to its western end. Shortly after crossing Abrams Creek Bridge, you'll see a road leading right and a marker indicating the Abrams Creek Parking Area. The trail starts at the parking area, which also is where Mill Creek, a major tributary, joins Abrams.

Much of the trail is easy, with a fairly even grade down close to the creek. However, at two or three points, the trail crosses piny ridges, while the creek makes wide detours around them, but you are always within sound of the rushing creek waters. As you top one of the hills, you'll be hearing the creek far down to your left rear. Then, after taking another step or two, as the trail twists to the right, you'll hear the creek roar from a different direction, your left front. A look at the map will show you that the creek traveled more than a mile, in a wide loop, from where you heard it two steps back to where you hear it now.

By the time Abrams Creek tumbles over Abrams Falls, it is carrying lots of water. It drops approximately 20 feet from the lip of the ledge to the dark pool below.

This is a good hike for any season. However, it is especially good for the second half of May. One reason is that trout season opens May 16. Another is that this is the usual time for laurel to bloom.

An odd thing about a laurel bloom is a method by which its pollen is scattered. You can help do the scattering. Notice the stamens, the small filaments coming up from the center of the flower. You'll see that the stamen ends, called the anthers, fit into tiny notches in the corolla, the inner portion of the single fused petal. Take a twig or pencil tip and dislodge an anther from its notch, and see the tiny shower of pollen. Insects normally do the task you did with the pencil.

Another good flower that blooms about the same time is sweet shrub, a small bush which has maroon flowers. Crush a flower or one of the leaves and smell the sweetness.

6 ALUM CAVE BLUFFS
4.5 miles, round trip
See No. 6 on map

This very popular hike is good at any season, but it is prettiest in early June, the normal time for rose-pink rhododendron to bloom.

The well-maintained trail leaves U. S. Highway 441 at the Alum Cave Bluffs Parking Area, about nine miles up the mountain from Park Headquarters at Gatlinburg. It crosses and recrosses Alum Cave Creek for the first 1.3 miles.

This little stream is unusually pretty, even for the Great Smokies. It is inhabited by brook trout. You can catch 'em but you can't keep 'em. For this is one of the Park's "fish-for-fun" streams. When you hook a fish, wet your hands in the water, gently take the fish off the hook and return him to the stream, uninjured if possible.

There is an exception. If you catch a fish 16 inches long or longer, you may keep it as a trophy. But your chances of catching a 16-inch brook trout in the Great Smokies are only a little better than for catching a whale in the Tennessee River. A 10-incher is a good brookie for the Smokies. But these rascals make up with beauty and fighting spirit what they lack in size. (The 16-inch rule on "fish-for-fun" streams also applies to rainbow and brown trout, and you may find one of these that big in some Park streams. But not in this one. Seven inches is the keeper limit for all Park streams other than the "fish-for-fun" ones.)

The trail winds through thick growth of white rhododendron (which normally blooms in late June or early July) before reaching a fine forest composed mostly of yellow birch and hemlock.

Creek and trail stay close together a short distance beyond Arch Rock.

This formation is what you'd expect—a great stone arch. The trail climbs through it on a flight of stone steps. The rock is black slate. The opening, now large enough for

14

persons to walk through with ease, started as a crack thousands of years ago. Weathering and frost action caused its growth.

Next important point of interest is a large heath bald through which the trail passes. Growing here are laurel, sand myrtle, a few blueberry bushes and a great deal of rose-pink rhododendron. It's the rhododendron that makes the splashy show. If the season is normal, the bloom is best June 5-15. It blooms a few days later higher up the mountain.

A heath bald sometimes is called a laurel slick, and mountaineers used to call them "laurel hells." They were hell to get through if there was no trail. The bushes grow in such a tight tangle that nothing much larger than a chipmunk can get through a laurel hell without cussing.

Not far beyond the heath bald, you get your first look at Alum Cave Bluffs. It's all bluff, not a cave. But what a bluff! This overhanging mountain of black slate could shelter hundreds. It is nearly 100 yards long, with an overhang of 20 to 25 yards at its widest point.

A marker tells one:

"This high overhanging cliff is the result of weathering of black slate at its base. This slate contains an abundance of iron sulfide; weak sulfuric acid formed by the weathering of the sulfide has decomposed the slate, resulting in the dust which covers the ground.

"Ground waters seeping through the rock have picked up a certain amount of mineral matter and deposited it on the face of the bluff in the form of alum. It is only a thin film and not of commercial importance. Nevertheless, a persistent legend has it that saltpeter was found here in considerable quantities during the Civil War and that it was converted into gunpowder."

(If you consider this hike too short, continue the same trail and you'll reach Mt. LeConte. See next hike.)

7 MT. LE CONTE

Suggested route, 13.2 miles, round trip
See No. 7 on map

This is the most popular destination in the Great Smokies for long hikers. The reasons are multiple.

Two of its peaks—Myrtle Point and Cliff Top—offer thrilling views of mountain wilderness. Each has a "specialty." Myrtle Point is for sunrises and Cliff Top is for sunsets.

However, unless you want to hike in darkness, seeing sunrise and sunset from these points requires spending the night on Le Conte. There is a variety of accommodations.

Le Conte Lodge can house about 50 guests very comfortably and a few others less comfortably. About twelve  can sleep in a Park Service shelter cabin, similar to those on the Appalachian Trail. Then, there is a primitive camping area. The Lodge provides good food for its guests. Bring your own if you intend to use the camping area or the shelter cabin.

At 6593 feet above sea level, Mt. Le Conte is the third highest peak in the Park, 50 feet lower than Clingmans Dome and 28 feet lower than Mt. Guyot. However, some Le Conte fans scorn this formula of comparison. They say Le Conte is the "tallest" peak east of the Rocky Mountains. They mean that it towers higher above its immediate base than does any other peak. The base, at Gatlinburg, is 1292 feet above sea level. That makes Le Conte a mile and 21 feet "tall." That's how much altitude you'll gain if you take the 13.2-mile hike from Gatlinburg, by way of Roaring Fork Creek and Trillium Gap, to Le Conte.

Le Conte Lodge is the highest resort east of the Mississippi River. Situated on a clearing in a forest of spruce and fir, it looks like a frontier outpost. Seven or eight balsam log cabins are guest sleeping quarters. Two large ones are three-bedroom buildings, with the bedrooms built in a half circle around a large livingroom. Each bedroom has a double-decker bed that sleeps four. A balsam log fire burns every night—and sometimes during the day—in the wide livingroom fireplace. It is always cool on Le Conte. The mercury has never been known to top 80 there.

A large shingled building houses the dining room and kitchen and the living quarters for the operators.

First man to operate a guest facility atop Le Conte was Paul Adams. Under contract with Great Smoky Mountains Conservation Association (which was backing establishment of a national park in the Great Smokies), Paul began operations in 1925. His first guests slept in a large tent. He later built a cabin. He started operations near the same spring that provides water for the present Le Conte Lodge. This spring is believed to be the highest constant-flow spring in Eastern North America. It is a few feet more than 6300 feet above sea level. (For an account of Paul's year on Le Conte, with his dog, Cumberland Jack, read his book, "Mt. Le Conte.")

Jack Huff, son of the late Andy Huff who built Gatlinburg's Mountain View Hotel, took over from Paul in 1926 and started developing the Lodge that is there today. Mr. Huff climbed Le Conte hundreds of times. One thing troubled him: His aging mother had never seen the world from Le Conte's lofty peaks. A semi-invalid, she was not able to hike or ride a horse.

So Jack fashioned a special chair which he could strap onto his back. And that's how he carried his 90-pound mother to Mt. Le Conte. He said she was the only person who ever went to Le Conte backwards.

Jack and his wife, Pauline, were married at sunrise on Myrtle Point, April, 1934. They operated the Lodge through the 1949 season, after which Jack had to operate the Mountain View, because of his father's death. Mrs. Huff, with a good staff to help, continued with the Lodge through the 1959 season. The Huffs then sold their interests to another couple who love the mountains, Mr. and Mrs. Herrick Brown. The Browns took over the Lodge in 1960, under a lease arrangement with the National Park Service.

Mrs. Brown soon learned that cooking on Le Conte has special problems. It takes 50 minutes to boil potatoes on Le Conte, compared with 20 minutes in Gatlinburg. Mrs. Huff years ago worked out a good recipe for Le Conte pancakes. Mrs. Brown still uses it.

The high altitude causes the culinary problem; the boiling point is low. Mrs. Brown says it's difficult to cook carrots. She has learned to French fry potatoes there, but they don't brown.

You probably will see bears on Le Conte. They hang around campgrounds, garbage cans along the highways—anywhere they're likely to find food left by humans. They sometimes raid the Lodge garbage pit. Don't feed them. If you don't have enough food to satisfy them, they'll get angry. Besides, you lower the dignity of a fine animal by making a panhandler of him. If you leave food in a tent or bedroll, you're inviting bear trouble. Hang food eight or nine feet high in a tree and at a point on a slender branch five or six feet from the trunk.

Cliff Top and Myrtle Point are rocky, nature-made platforms, with views of hundreds of square miles of mountains and distant lowlands. The lights of Knoxville and smaller East Tennessee towns are visible on clear nights.

Though virtually treeless, Cliff Top and Myrtle Point have thick patches of the small Carolina rhododendron and the shorter sand myrtle. Sand myrtle is a little evergreen with glossy leaves not much larger than a mouse's ear and pretty pink-white blooms. It usually blooms in the first half of June at this altitude, while the Carolina rhododendron blooms a little later.

Myrtle Point is nearly a mile from the Lodge. It is reached by crossing High Top, Le Conte's highest point. Though a little higher than Cliff Top and Myrtle Point, High Top offers no good view because it is covered with trees. Cliff Top is about a quarter of a mile from the Lodge.

A good early-morning routine, particularly for a bird watcher, is to get out of bed in time to reach Myrtle Point for the sunrise scene. Make the return slowly. Breakfast isn't nearly ready. Take a side hike a quarter of a mile out the Boulevard Trail. You'll hear the haunting song of the veery and the long, lovely song of the winter wren. Only a careful birder can get a look at the shy veery, but you can see the stub-tailed little wren sitting on the tip top of a tree. Other birds you may see include robins, Carolina juncos, red-breasted nuthatches, golden-crowned kinglets, solitary vireos, and chestnut-sided, blackthroated blue, Canada and Blackburnian warblers. The warblers, the veery and the vireo are only summer residents at this latitude.

The Carolina junco and his close kin, the slate-colored junco, winter in the East Tennessee lowlands, as well as in other places. They look so much alike that only an expert can tell which is which. However, when spring comes, the slate-colored junco flies 1000 miles north to Canada, to a

18

land of spruce and fir and birch and fire cherry. And the Carolina junco flies four or five miles to the top of the Great Smokies, also a land of spruce and fir and birch and fire cherry.

Five major trails lead to Le Conte. The shortest, one way, is 5.2 miles, the longest, 11.2. For those who have two cars, or who can otherwise arrange transportation, I'd suggest going by way of Alum Cave Bluff (discussed in Hike No. 6), 5.2 miles, and returning by way of the Boulevard Trail, 8 miles. The latter follows the high Boulevard Ridge southward to the main crest of the Great Smokies. From there, hikers follow the Appalachian Trail westward to Newfound Gap. From the Boulevard one can see some of the ruggedest regions of the Great Smokies.

Those who have only one car but who want to ascend and descend by different trails can leave from Cherokee Orchard and take the Rainbow Falls Trail, 6.75 miles, and return on the Bullhead Trail, 7 miles. The Bullhead offers magnificant autumn scenery.

Another fine trail is the one by way of Trillium Gap. Grotto Falls, on Roaring Fork Creek, spills its cold water smack into the trail. To keep dry, walk behind the falls, next to the rock ledge. To reach the best starting point for this trail, leave the Cherokee Orchard Loop Road and take the one-way Roaring Fork Motor Nature Trail. Follow it about 1.7 miles. Look for a trail marker about one-tenth of a mile beyond the first bridge on the road. However, as of this writing, the gates at the beginning and ending of the Roaring Fork motor trail are locked at night, and one is not permitted to leave a car by the road overnight. So keep this in mind when planning your hike.

On the Trillium Gap Trail, listen for underground streams rumbling through the rocks between Grotto Falls and Trillium Gap. (In times of dry weather, Roaring Fork Creek goes underground for a long stretch, a mile or more off the trail, above Grotto Falls.) Interesting features of the Rainbow Falls Trail are the falls, where Le Conte Creek takes a mighty leap, and Rocky Spur, good for rose-pink rhododendron. The Bullhead heath bald is fine for spring blooms and contrasting fall colors on the Bullhead Trail.

In a recent season the Lodge housed 4276 overnight guests. Many others hiked to Le Conte and returned the same day or camped overnight on top. Nearly all who go to Le Conte reach it on foot. Mr. Brown estimates that only about 5 per cent ride horses. Ages of hikers have varied from less than four to 85. The Browns' daughter Barbara hiked all the way up the Alum Cave Trail when she was less than three and a half years old.

19

8 GREGORY BALD

Suggested routes, 10.5, 12, or 13.3 miles, round trip
See No. 8 on map

If you can hike only once to Gregory Bald, go when the flame azaleas bloom. Best time usually is June 15-25. Before you go, though, check with Park officials to learn whether the bloom is on schedule.

The "most gay and brilliant flowering shrub yet known" was William Bartram's description of flame azaleas. **Mr.** Bartram, first botanist to visit the Great Smokies, had his first look at flame azaleas in 1776.

Go to Gregory and you probably will agree with him. Hundreds, probably thousands, of azaleas bloom there. They are white, pink, yellow, orange and a striking orange-red. Most numerous are the orange and yellow.

Gregory is the second or third largest of several balds in the Great Smokies. There are two types—grass balds and heath balds. Gregory is classed as a grass bald because grass is its predominant cover. A heath bald is one thickly

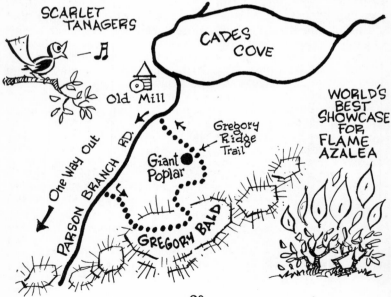

covered with heath plants—mostly laurel and rhododendron.

How the grass balds came to be is a mystery. Fire and grazing have been advanced as possible reasons why the forest which covers the surrounding area does not also cover them. Indians said the gods cleared them.

Dr. Randolph Shields, a botanist who was born and reared in Cades Cove, below Gregory, says the bald area has dwindled considerably since he herded sheep and cattle there in his youth. Back then, the Cove dwellers summered their herds on Gregory and two other large grass balds, Spence Field and Russell Field. Livestock fattened well on the lush wild grass.

The forest has crept upward year by year since the land became part of the Park and grazing was stopped, in the early 1930s. This place of grass and flowers now contains only about a dozen acres. Dr. Shields says it was several times that large when he herded on it.

Azaleas grow thickest in a fringe around the edge of the bald, where the grass and forest meet. However, they are scattered all over, along with a few blueberry and serviceberry bushes. Most of these azaleas are thickly branched, sturdy and rather squat, compared with slender, taller ones that grow in the woods along the trails to Gregory.

Gregory is 4949 feet above sea level at its highest point, but the bald area extends down to about the 4800-foot contour line.

If you are thirsty and have no water, try an azalea gall. They are greenish-white, about the size of a baby's hand, and they grow on azalea branches. Most persons aren't really fond of them, however, some are. They have little taste, but what they do have reminds one faintly of that part of a watermelon where the red fades into the white-green rind. They're full of liquid.

If you dislike the galls, you can still thwart a thirst. Moore's Spring, said to be the best in the mountains, is only about a half mile from the bald. A good shelter cabin stands near it.

How to get to Gregory:

Two trails lead there from the Cades Cove area. A narrow motor road breaks off the Cades Cove loop road, only a few feet beyond the entrance to the Cable Mill. Follow it to where it dead ends at a turn-around.   The Gregory Ridge Trail starts at the turn-around.

The other trail is the Hannah Mountain Trail.   Reach it by following the same motor road, but turn right off it onto the Parson Branch Road and follow the latter three miles to the Hannah Mountain Trail at Sams Gap.

A word of caution: In your planning, remember the Parson Branch Road is one-way.   The gates at both ends are closed at night.   If you intend to make a loop hike— going by one trail and returning by the other, you may as well plan to walk the Parson Branch Road, leaving your car outside the gate.   The alternative is to have a friend pick you up at the end of the hike.

If you walk the road and make the loop hike, your round trip is 13.3 miles.   If you ascend and descend the Hannah Mountain Trail, leaving your car on the Parson Branch Road, your round trip is about nine miles.   If you go and return by the Gregory Ridge Trail, the round trip is about 12 miles.   If you go by Gregory Ridge and return by Hannah Mountain, having someone to meet you at the end of the trail, your round trip is about 10.5 miles.

If you ascend and descend by the same route, I suggest the Gregory Ridge Trail.   This is because you should not miss the exceptional beauty of the first mile or two of this trail, in Forge Creek Valley.   Magnificent hemlock and tulip trees grow here.   One of them is the so-called Giant Poplar.

I recall going up one of the trails and coming back on the other with Mr. and Mrs. Arthur Stupka and Dr. Shields. Mr. Stupka, park naturalist for many years and later Park biologist, is an authority on everything that blooms, walks, crawls, flies and sings in the mountains.   He's particularly good on birds.

And he was working birds this misty morning on the Hannah Mountain Trail.   He listened for their songs, often checking the altimeter he carried and making notes on the altitudes at which he first heard various species.   We listened to simultaneous serenades from a scarlet tanager and a rose-breasted grosbeak.   We saw three or four of each. The scarlet tanager is to birddom in the Eastern United States what Bartram said of flame azaleas—the "most gay and brilliant."

We startled a junco which had a nest on the ground in a thick patch of wood betony beside the trail.   She left in such a hurry that she kicked one of her four mottled eggs from the nest.   Mrs. Stupka found the nest and put back the egg.

22

9 MT. CAMMERER
11.5 miles, round trip
See No. 9 on map

A magnificent view from the top and the forest and flowers along the way make this long jaunt worthwhile. The altitude gain is 2928 feet—from 2000 feet above sea level at the Davenport Gap starting point to 4928 at Mt. Cammerer Tower.

Most Americans today think a hike this long is ridiculous or impossible. "Sport," for many of us, is sitting in the stadium and watching somebody else play. And television is making the trip to the stadium unnecessary.

However, some remain who are of tougher fiber. I met a family of them atop Mt. Cammerer on the last day of June, 1961. The first person I saw was a little girl, curled up on a rock ledge outside the fire tower, sleeping. Resting on the platform that encircles the tower were Dr. and Mrs. Robert P. Madden, Alexandria, Va., and two of their three children, Carl 2½ years, and Donnie, 9. The third child was the one sleeping outside, 6-year-old Debbie. She was curing an upset stomach with a nap. Dr. Madden, a lean young physicist, had carried Carl most of the way. All except Debbie had made the hike OK.

Mt. Cammerer offers one of the five or six best views in the Park. The fire tower perches high on a rugged, treeless ledge of gray-white rock. Because of the light color of the stone, which can be seen for miles, the peak was once called Whiterock. Quite unlike the customary fire tower, with a cab atop a tall steel framework, this tower is a squat building of wood and stone, encircled by a wooden platform.

Look from here at hundreds of square miles of fields and forests. To the north and east lie the farm lands of Cocke County, Tenn., with Pigeon River curving lazily through them. To the west runs the main range of the Great Smokies, with 6621-foot Mt. Guyot, second highest peak in the Park, dominating the scene. Stretching away to the south are the forested mountains of the North Carolina

23

side of the Park; another fire tower is visible on Mt. Sterling five miles south.

The approach road to Davenport Gap, starting point of the hike, is State Highway 32 on the Tennessee side. The road hugs the eastern Park boundary most of the way. On the opposite side of the road are mountain farms and farm buildings. The road has a good paved surface but is narrow and crooked. The approach from North Carolina is State 284, narrow, crooked and unpaved.

For nearly a mile, the trail is a jeep road, leading to a shelter cabin. Leave this road before it reaches the shelter and take the foot trail angling to the left.

Plants and trees are varied. The two major types of rhododendron—rosebay or great white rhododendron and Catawba or rose-pink rhododendron—are well represented. The white grows at the lower elevation and the trail tunnels through a long thick mass of it. Growing high on Mt. Cammerer's slopes is the rose-pink, lovely against the light-colored rock. The rose-pink normally blooms best around the middle of June. The white blooms the first part of July.

Much laurel grows along the southern slopes of the middle section of the trail, in a sparse forest of pines, oaks, red maples, sourwoods, blackgums. and a few chestnut sprouts. Except for the pines, these trees have bright autumn colors.

Look for table mountain pine. Its cones grow in circles of three or four around the branches. They are the spiniest, heaviest pine cones in the region, and are so tough that they sometimes take years to open and release their seeds. Table mountain pine branches are exceptionally pliant and difficult to break.

You usually will find wintergreen, sometimes called mountain tea, in this type of woodland. It is a low-growing evergreen plant, and its leaves resemble laurel leaves, except they are slightly smaller. The old leaves have a pleasant aromatic flavor, but the new spring leaves are somewhat bitter. Don't chew them unless you are certain it is wintergreen and not laurel; for laurel leaves bring nothing but grief to anyone who chews them. In the fall, wintergreen has small red berries which are sweeter than the leaves.

At about the 4500-foot elevation, you will enter a fine forest which has much eastern hemlock and yellow birch. And above this is the spruce-fir forest which grows at the highest elevations of the Great Smokies.

There are two trail intersections after you leave the jeep road. A trail to the right, about half way to the top, goes to Cosby Campground. At the top, a jeep road to the right takes you to the tower.

To the left of the trail, about a quarter of a mile beyond the Cosby trail intersection, is a spring. It is not visible from the trail, and you may miss the path to it if you are not alert. One or two other springs provide very cold water near the top of the mountain.

Here are two good alternate routes to Mt. Cammerer:

9-a. Hike southward out of Cosby Campground 2.5 miles to Low Gap, on the Tennessee-Carolina line. Then turn eastward on the Appalachian Trail to Cammerer. Total mileage is a little less than 5.5.

9-b. Drive Tennessee Highway 32 about 3.6 miles southeastward from intersection of 32 and Tennessee 73, at Cosby. Or, if you are leaving from Cosby Campground, follow 32 about 2.3 miles southeastward from intersection of 32 and campground entrance road. Starting point of hike is an old road whose entrance to cars is blocked by a park gate. Follow old road about a mile to where it ends in a cul-de-sac. Take a trail off cul-de-sac. Follow trail about a half-mile to where it joins an east-west trail. Turn left on that trail and follow it about 3.5 miles to an intersection with the Appalachian Trail. Turn right on AT and follow it about three more miles to Cammerer. Total mileage, about eight.

Hiking groups with access to two or more cars may want to go to Cammerer by one of these routes and return by another.

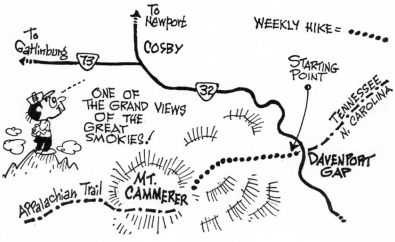

10 RAMSAY CASCADE

5 miles, round trip

See No. 10 on map

Here's a drive and then a walk through a forest of big trees and along lively streams. The drive is along Middle Prong of Little Pigeon River, and the walk is along Ramsay Prong, a Middle Prong tributary. The destination is one of the most refreshing places in the mountains on a hot summer day.

The route: Leave State Highway 73 at the bridge across Middle Prong. Follow the narrow Park road upstream past the ranger's residence and past a temporary campground. Look for Ramsay Cascade markers where the road forks, one road continuing up the right side of a stream and the other turning abruptly left across the stream. Your road is the one to the left. Notice the scattered large boulders in the creek.

There are three gates on the motor road to the starting point of the hike. The Park Service locks one of them from 8 p.m. to 8 a.m. throughout the year, and keeps it locked throughout the day during periods of bad weather. Park practice varies as to which gate is locked.

If the lower gate, at Greenbrier Ranger Station, is locked, forget this hike. The distance is too great for most and the long walk along the gravel road is not particularly rewarding. The second gate is just across the bridge from where Porters Creek joins Middle Prong. Round-trip distance from there is 12 miles. The third gate is a mile up the road, leaving a round-trip walking distance of 10 miles. It usually is best to make this hike only when the road is open all the way to where it ends and the trail starts. Leave your car at the parking area near the turn-around. This is only a few yards from the confluence of Ramsay Prong and Buck Fork and it's 2.5 miles to the Cascade.

Except for a stretch of about one-half mile, the trail winds close to the stream, and hikers will enjoy some lovely mountain stream scenes. They also will notice other scenes typical of these high mountain valleys, with their heavy rainfall and temperate climate.

See how quickly ferns and other small plants and even trees start growing on fallen tree trunks—on some even before they fall. After crossing the second footbridge turn and look back at the horizontal branch of the tree growing near the other end of the bridge. Though it is 10 to 12 feet above ground, it is covered with ferns—sort of an aerial fernery.

Keep watch to the left of the trail for a huge tulip poplar, a few inches more than 18 feet in circumference at chest height. It is one of the three or four largest known trees in the Park.

Look for trees with "prop roots." Many years ago, a seed sprouted in an old tree stump. Roots of the new tree grew through the old stump to the ground. Gradually the stump decayed, leaving the new tree with its roots extending two or three feet above ground. Also, look at trees that similarly grew from seeds that sprouted on large rocks. Unlike the stumps, the rocks did not decay. So the tree roots, like claws, clutch the rocks.

Ramsay Cascade is a high and mighty splash of white water down a craggy-faced ledge which is nearly vertical and 75 or more feet high. It hits a dozen rocky noses and chins on the way down and pauses at none of them. It tempers its pace on a broad stone ledge, a few foot above the footbridge which is at the foot of the falls. The ledge is a wonderful place to lie on one's back in the sunshine and be sprinkled with chilling spray from the cascading water. The ledge itself is refreshingly cool to the skin on a hot summer day. The view down the narrow green valley is pleasant. So is the view of the white water crashing down over the rocks above.

* * * * * *

While you may eat berries you find in the Park, it is a violation of Park regulations to remove or damage any plants or animals.

11 SILERS BALD — CLINGMANS DOME
10 miles, round trip
See No. 11 on map

Nearly all this trail is more than a mile high, and it's an exciting hike you'll long remember.

The first leg is a long half mile, from the Forney Ridge Parking Area to Clingmans Dome Tower. At 6643 feet above sea level, the Dome is the highest point in the Park and the second highest east of the Mississippi River. The tower gives it an additional 45 feet. From the tower, one can see for miles in every direction on a clear day.

However, I remember a July morning when the sky was not clear. To the contrary, the atmosphere was a sea of mist. It was like trying to look through acres of filmy

gauze. The mist was so fine I could not feel it falling. But it collected in droplets on the hairs of my forearms. It collected on the needles of the spruce and fir trees and fell from them in a steady drip, drip, drip. From out of the mist came the veery's eerie song and the lovely notes of a winter wren.

After coming down from the tower, take the narrow trail to the right and follow it a few feet to the Appalachian Trail which will take you westward to Silers Bald.

A quarter of a mile westward is a razorback section of trail barely wide enough to hold the Tennessee-North Carolina boundary. It is followed by a large semi-bald area which is very impressive.

This is a world with a different look. Trees on the bald are gnarled and small and few, but grass and weeds grow thickly and about a foot high. There are great patches of thornless blackberries. Late in the season though it was, the blackberries were in full bloom. Blackberries in the lowlands were ripe then.

Also blooming were large purple-fringed orchis (Habenaria fibriata). Though this flower is fairly rare in the Great Smokies, I counted more than 80 on this bald. They're very pretty.

Somewhere down this ragged slope, you may see Turk's cap lilies. Their huge orange-red blooms are dotted with brown. Petals are recurving. Good specimens grow eight feet tall and have up to a dozen blooms. They normally bloom in late July, and I have seen them blooming then, but not on this particular trip, for the season was a late one.

From the bald area, the trail goes back into woodland, composed mostly of spruce and fir but with some beech and yellow birch.

Look for the Double Springs Gap marker. The springs are 50 yards apart. One is 15 yards off the trail on the North Carolina side and the other 35 yards inside Tennessee.

Five or six quail-sized young ruffed grouse exploded into the air from near the Tennessee spring when I approached. Their mother quickly followed. (These were the first of more than a dozen grouse I saw on this hike.) A few seconds later, a large hawk sailed through the trees. He probably had had a luncheon interest in the young grouse.

Several yards west of the gap was another fellow who may have had the same interest. This was a red fox. He saw me and raced ahead along the trail and out of sight around a curve. I soon saw him again, still on the trail, and he ran ahead again. I saw him no more till I was on the return trip, and then only once.

Red foxes are indigenous to these highlands, while gray foxes like the lowlands better. However, some red foxes now are found in the lowlands because fox hunters have imported them and turned them loose there.

Another highland animal you may see is the little red squirrel called the "boomer." You won't find him in the lowlands of East Tennessee, but you would find him, or some of his close kin, in similar spruce-fir forests of Canada and New England.

A low-growing flower you'll see under thick stands of spruce and fir is mountain sorrel (Oxalis montana), sometimes called wood shamrock It has three leaves and a small white bloom threaded with pink. It can thrive under the spruce and fir because it requires very little sunlight.

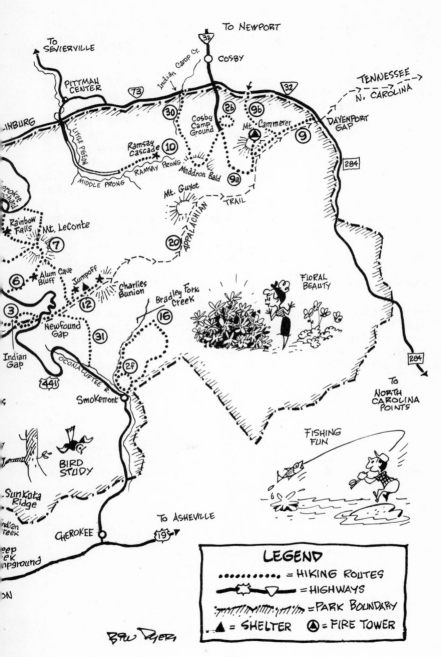

TO NEWPORT

TO SEVIERVILLE

PITTMAN CENTER

LINBURG

COSBY

32

Indian Camp Cr.

73

30

Cosby Camp Ground

2b

9b

Mt. Cammerer

32

TENNESSEE →
N. CAROLINA

DAVENPORT GAP

9

284

Ramsay Cascade

10

Ramsay Prong

Maddron Bald

9a

Little Pigeon

MIDDLE PRONG

Mt. Guyot

APPALACHIAN

TRAIL

Cherokee

Rainbow Falls

Mt. LeConte

7

6

Alum Cave Bluff

Jumpoff

Charlies Bunion

12

20

FLORAL BEAUTY

3

Newfound Gap

31

16

Bradley Fork Creek

Indian Gap

441

OCONALUFTEE R.

2f

Smokemont

To
NORTH CAROLINA POINTS

284

s

BIRD STUDY

FISHING FUN

Sunkota Ridge

ndian reek

CHEROKEE

TO ASHEVILLE

19

eep ek mpground

ON

LEGEND

••••••••••	= HIKING ROUTES
▬▬◇▬▽▬	= HIGHWAYS
⌇⌇⌇⌇⌇⌇	= PARK BOUNDARY
▲	= SHELTER Ⓐ = FIRE TOWER

BI11 DYER

31

The first bald you reach west of Double Springs Gap is a small one, decorated with a few flame azalea and laurel bushes. But this is not Silers. You have more walking.

Not far beyond the small bald is the Narrows, a rocky section where the mountain crest is little wider than the trail. This is the only part of the hike where the altitude dips a few feet below a mile.

The trail forks at the foot of Silers. The left fork angles down Welch Ridge and the right one climbs Silers. The climb to the top of Silers is steep but mercifully short.

Silers is a large bald, mostly grassy but with some blackberries and a few heath plants. The elevation at the top is 5607 feet. Go down the western slope to the Appalachian Trail shelter. A good spring is near.

Take a good rest. The way back is long and often steep.

Return by the same route, except for the last half mile. At the trail forks, take the lower fork, to Forney Ridge Parking Area, rather than the left one to the Dome. Turn left at the next trail intersection, and follow the trail through an area of tremendous boulders to the parking area.

(If you want a short loop hike of less than two miles, rather than the long one to Silers, do only the first and last legs of the long hike. Go to the tower, get on the Appalachian Trail and follow it down to the first marked intersection. Turn sharply left. Turn left again at the next intersection and go back to your car.)

* * * * * *

No place of equal size in the United States has as many kinds of salamanders as Great Smoky Mountains National Park, where more than two dozen species live. One of these, Jordan's salamander, has been found only in the Park.

* * * * * *

The U. S. Fish and Wildlife Service lists 72 species of fishes in Great Smokies streams. However, fishermen are chiefly interested in trout in these streams. There are a few bass and sunfishes. The Fish and Wildlife Service and the Park Service list 333 streams and 734.6 fishable miles in the Park.

12 CHARLIES BUNION and the JUMPOFF
Bunion, 8 mi., round trip; Jumpoff, 6.5 mi., round trip
Bunion and Jumpoff, 11 mi., round trip
See No. 12 on map

Both of these places offer spectacular views. Though it is almost vertical, the Jumpoff is clothed with vegetation. Not so Charlies Bunion. It is as steep as the Jumpoff, but it is mostly bare rock. The two places are only about a mile apart, as the raven flies, and each can be seen from the other.

This doesn't mean you have to reach both on the same hike. They're presented together here because much of the trail is the same to both.

Follow the Appalachian Trail eastward from Newfound Gap. You'll soon be away from the sound of automobiles and the smell of exhaust fumes, and you'll be walking through a forest of red spruce and fir trees, cool and dimly lighted on the hottest, brightest days.

Trees, flowers, ferns, mosses and lichens cover nearly every inch of all except the trail. Rainfall is heavy. Rhododendron and other shrubs grow out of rock ledges where very little soil is visible.

However, nature is not always a constructive builder. Look a few miles northward at the great scars on the south slope of Mt. Le Conte. These were left by a Labor Day weekend flash flood in 1951. It may be a century before nature's more gentle hand restores what she swept away here in one fierce hour.

Spruce and fir are found much more in Canada than in this latitude. The cool temperatures at the high-altitude crest of the Great Smokies permit their growth. Here's how to distinguish spruce from fir:

Spruce grows larger. It has short, sharp needles that are green all over. Fir has larger needles which are flat,

33

green on top and white on the bottom. Spruce bark is scaly but fir bark is smooth. You'll see more moss on fir bark, because the scales drop off the spruce bark, carrying the moss with them. Fir bark is covered with small blisters. Burst one with a thumbnail and taste the resin that pops out.

You'll find flowers blooming along this trail any time between the frost seasons. One that's numerous in late summer is the touch-me-not, ranging in color from yellow to nearly white. Touch a touch-me-not seed pod and you'll find how it got its name. The pod bursts open and the seeds are scattered.

Two and a half miles east of Newfound Gap, the trail forks. The left fork is the Boulevard Trail, to Mt. Le Conte. The right one continues as the Appalachian Trail.

To reach the Jumpoff, take the Boulevard Trail for a few yards, looking, as you walk, for the marker that will put you on the narrow Jumpoff trail that angles to the right. It's a rough trail but not a dangerous one if you are reasonably careful.

You'll soon be going through a large blackberry patch. These high-mountain blackberry canes are virtually thornless. Their small, seedy berries ripen in late August or September.

From the blackberry thicket, the trail winds along a spruce-fir razorback ridge and reaches the Jumpoff. You'll see outcropping slate layers pointed skyward. Down to the right for a thousand feet there is nothing much but fresh air and a view.

Although the cliff wall plunges nearly straight down, it is clothed with shrubs and small trees. The little Carolina rhododendron seems to be the dominant cliffhanger.

If you're a bird watcher, don't forget your glasses on this trip. You'll see many small birds, including several warblers, fliting along almost directly below you. And you may see a raven or a hawk.

To go to Charlies Bunion, continue on the Appalachian Trail. A good resting place not far from the trail fork is the AT shelter at Ice Water Spring.

In 1925, before the Park was established, a fire killed much of the vegetation on the peak that later was called Charlies Bunion. A flash flood hit the same area four years later. With the anchoring tree roots killed by the fire, the soil on the Tennessee side was washed away by the flood. Spectacular bare rock remains.

According to Paul Fink, in his "The Names and Lore of the Great Smokies," a group of North Carolinians hiked to the top of the mountain to see what damage the flood had done. In the group was Charlie Connor, a man who had long suffered from an unusually large bunion. Looking at the bare-rock knob, one of the others said, "That sticks out like Charlie's bunion."

* * * * * *

More than 100 tree species grow in the Great Smokies — more than in any other national park, more than two-thirds as many as grow in all Europe, and probably more than in any other area of similar size (507,000 acres) in North America. The Park has 18 tree "champions," the largest known of their species. They are as follows, with trunk girth given for four and one-half feet above ground:

1. *Yellow birch, 14 feet, one inch.*
2. *Mountain ash, five feet, six inches.*
3. *Yellow buckeye, 15 feet, 11 inches.*
4. *Devil's walkingstick, two feet, three inches.*
5. *Fraser fir, seven feet, nine inches.*
6. *Eastern hemlock, 19 feet, 10 inches.*
7. *American hornbeam, seven feet, seven inches.*
8. *Cucumber magnolia, 18 feet, four inches.*
9. *Fraser magnolia, nine feet, three inches.*
10. *Mountain laurel, three feet, six inches.*
11. *Mountain maple, three feet.*
12. *Table mountain pine, six feet, 11 inches.*
13. *Serviceberry, six feet, two and one-half inches.*
14. *Silverbell, 11 feet, nine inches.*
15. *Sourwood, seven feet, seven inches.*
16. *Red spruce, 14 feet, one inch.*
17. *Winterberry, one foot, nine inches.*
18. *Hazel alder, one foot, 10 inches.*

13 BLANKET MOUNTAIN

Approximately 10 miles

See No. 13 on map

My wife and son made this hike with me one autumn day we won't forget. It's a trans-mountain jaunt from Little River Valley, at Elkmont, up Jakes Creek and over Blanket Mountain, then down to Middle Prong of Little River and down that valley to the gate above the Tremont Ranger Station.

Alberta is not a frequent hiker, and son Kit was only nine. Nevertheless, they were in pretty good condition at the end of the hike. Kit nearly wore out a pair of shoes, though.

You'll need two cars. We left one at the gate above Tremont. We went to Elkmont in the other and left it at the start of the Jakes Creek Trail.

This is a good hike any time between early spring and late fall. We made it in early October, when the trail was covered with a brown and yellow carpet of new-fallen leaves.

We were soon passing through a second-growth forest of tulip poplars, straight trunked and beautifully mottled with green and yellowing leaves. Sunlight danced upon the leaves, suffusing the forest with sulphury light.

Look along this trail for occasional stands of black cherry trees. They generally are straight and tall and have very dark bark. Outside the Park, these trees are cut and the lumber is used for fine furniture.

Asters bloomed along the trail.

Kit was full of coltish energy. He tried to swing on grapevines, succeeding on some and pulling others down on top of him. He got into poison ivy somewhere, judging from the looks of his face and stomach a day or two later.

Another vine you'll see is Dutchman's pipe. It likes rich soil and isn't nearly as numerous as grapevine. It has light colored bark and large heart-shaped leaves.

Autumn color doesn't always mean the big picture of mountains covered with red and yellow leaves. It can be a tiny thing, such as the "doll's eyes" we saw on this trip.

The plant has a bright red branched fruit stalk, with white berries at the end of each branch. The red and white combination is striking.

What with grape-vine swinging, rock throwing and walking, Kit tired and started asking "How much farther?" before we reached Jakes Gap, four miles from the starting point. We rested briefly at the Gap, before turning right on the one-mile dead-end trail that goes to the top of Blanket Mountain.

This Blanket Mountain mile is dry. It has stunted pines and oaks, sourwoods, chestnut sprouts, huckleberries, laurel, rhododendron, mountain tea, trailing arbutus. Many gentians were blooming then. Sourwood and chestnut leaves gave red and yellow color to the trail.

The tea berries had just turned red. Kit and I ate several. And, even at this late date, a few tangy huckleberries were still on the bushes. A clump or two of witch hazel had started blooming.

The laurel and trailing arbutus make this a good spring hike.

Blanket Mountain's summit once was the site of a fire tower. But only the stone foundation of the lookout's cabin remains. Without the tower, the view from the top is not outstanding. There are better places a few yards back down the trail to stop and do some looking. Climb to the top of one of the large gray boulders beside the trail and look for miles out across the main range of the Great Smokies.

We went back to Jakes Gap and ate lunch.

Then we took the Catamount Creek Trail. (Catamount is another name for panther or mountain lion. The same animal is called a cougar in the Northwest and a puma in the Southwest. It roamed the mountains of East Tennessee years ago. A few persons insist it now is making a comeback here. Some say they've seen and heard panthers in the Norris Lake section, and also in the Tellico area of Cherokee National Forest. But most naturalists and game biologists are skeptical of the reports.)

The trail is pleasant. It stays close to Catamount Creek, a pretty mountain stream. The trail forks, without benefit of a marker, a short distance before it reaches Middle Prong. On a guess, we took the left fork of the trail. It turned out to be the correct one. We soon crossed Catamount Creek for the last time, and then reached Middle Prong, which we crossed on rocks, without getting our feet more than damp.

Next came a beautiful two or three miles down a good park road, always within sight and sound of Middle Prong. It is an excellent mountain stream, with alternating deep, green pools and white water that races down cascades and jumps down falls.

Wild grapevines grow everywhere in Middle Prong Valley. And the grape leaves were turning rust colored on this October afternoon.

* * * * * *

What makes leaf color? Pigments. Scientists say chlorophyll is the pigment that makes them green in spring and summer. Carotene, xanthophyll and anthocyanin give them their autumn colors.

* * * * * *

Black bear cubs are about the size of rats when they are born in January. They are much larger by the time the mother brings them out of hibernation, usually in March or April.

* * * * * *

About 300 bears live in the Park. A bear lives 15 or 20 years. An average adult bear weighs 200 to 350 pounds, and may reach 550 pounds when plenty of natural food is available.

14 COVE MOUNTAIN

Suggested route, 8.4 miles, round trip; Alternate trip, 13.2 miles, round trip; Horse trail, 18 miles, round trip

See No. 14 on map

Look down from Cove Mountain Fire Tower upon colors of autumn—blood-red of sourwoods, red and yellows of maples, mottled brown and yellow of tulip poplars and bright red of blackgums and scarlet oaks.

All these—plus pastels of sassafras and the dark-hued small leaves of low-growing huckleberry bushes—are yours to see on a hike to Cove Mountain in October. Colors often remain good into November.

Suggested route is from Fighting Creek Gap, on State Highway 73. Laurel Falls, a popular spot, is on this route. Return the same way. The alternate route is for persons who can make a two-car arrangement with friends. Leave one car at Fighting Creek Gap and the other at Park Headquarters, just above Gatlinburg. Follow a jeep road from there to the fire tower and take the Laurel Falls route back to the car at Fighting Creek Gap. Or if you want to ride a horse, take the route from Park headquarters and return the same way. (Horses are not permitted on the other trail.)

The long views from the fire tower are good. Look northwest at the abrupt east end of Chilhowee Mountain, which has blossomed into an attractive summer residential community. If you look westward, you can see the Foothills Parkway winding on or near the crest of the Chilhowees. To the south is the main range of the Great Smokies.

First leg of the hike, from Fighting Creek Gap to Laurel Falls, is one of the most popular in the park. Though good any season of the year, it is particularly attractive in spring and fall. Laurel and a few flame azalea bushes bloom in late May along that mile-and-a-quarter stretch.

Laurel Branch is one wild waterfall after another from high in the mountain almost to the point where it enters Little River. Laurel Falls is the most spectacular of its many jumps. The trail crosses the branch on a great shelf of rock at about the middle of the falls.

At one place on the trail, below the falls, one gets a good view of Blanket Mountain. (See Hike No. 13)

The Laurel Falls hike is so popular that the trail had to be paved. One usually sees several persons on it. I once saw a man riding a motorcycle on it. But if a Park ranger had seen him, he would have been in trouble. Motorcycles are illegal on Park trails. Hikers are permitted on all trails, and horseback riders are permitted on some.

The section of trail I like best is a half-mile to a mile above Laurel Falls. Here is virgin forest. Giant poplars and hemlocks and big yellow birches are numerous. Loggers cut over most of Cove Mountain before it was purchased for the Park. But, for some reason, they missed this section of fine trees.

* * * * * *

The cove hardwood forests of the Great Smokies are among the finest deciduous woodlands in the world. These trees resemble forests that grew here 20,000,000 years ago.

15 RICH MOUNTAIN FIRE TOWER
4 miles, round trip
See No. 15 on map

This short hike is good for spring flowers and fall colors. The drive to the trail start is delightful. Let's get that route out of the way first:

Follow the Cades Cove loop road about 3.2 miles to the one-way road which leads to the right from the loop road, at a point opposite the Cades Cove Missionary Baptist Church. Then follow this pleasant—though unimproved—mountain road approximately 2.9 miles to the point where the trail to the fire tower turns abruptly to the right off the road. There is a small parking space on the left side of the road.

Many wild flowers grow on Rich Mountain. And three are particularly pretty. All three grow in sandy, poor soil.

First is trailing arbutus. It has clusters of pink or white blooms in March, April and sometimes May. It grows along the trail. Second is bird's foot violet, which blooms in April. It grows along the road banks and probably along the trail, but I haven't been on the trail at the time it blooms. Third is the gentian, a September-October bloomer. This is one of the closed gentians. It may be white or blue, or white streaked with blue.

If you really appreciate the mountains, don't delay a hike you've planned just because the day happens to be foggy, or even a bit rainy. Arthur Stupka and I had a pleasant hike to Rich Mountain one fall day when fog was so dense that it nearly hid the cab atop the Rich Mountain fire tower from our view on the ground. We didn't bother to climb the tower.

The fog muted the brightness of the autumn leaves. However, if you think that's something to complain about, look some time at a bright scarlet oak leaf through a film of fog.

A damp day is better for those who like the fragrance of the forest. Dampness sharpens the sense of smell. A hunting dog tracks better on a damp day, and a dog on a chase sometimes will lick his nose to make it work better.

My wife and I made the same hike two days later. The fog was gone. The sky was blue. Colors were flamboyant,

41

and the view was for miles. At the invitation of the fire lookout, I went up into his cab for a look in all directions.

Colors shimmered in the sunlight down Rich Mountain toward Cades Cove. Red maples battled scarlet oaks and sourwoods in a war of the reds. White oaks were turning russet. Chestnut oaks and black oaks wore less brilliant hues. Sassafras leaves ranged from lemon to rust. Hickories, tulip poplars and some of the maples wore yellow. These colors marched down to the Cove and into it in fingers of woodland.

Stretched far to the east and south was the main range of the Great Smokies, visible from Clingmans Dome to Thunderhead, to Gregory Bald and still farther westward. Nearly 20 miles to the east, standing out by itself to the north of the main range, was Mt. Le Conte. Visible in the middle distance were Blanket Mountain and Cove Mountain.

Down on the ground again, the most striking color combination for close looking was provided by sourwoods— slender fingers of drying seed pods, nearly white, against the blood-red leaves.

When you return to the car, continue driving in the same direction. This is the old road to Townsend, and this is where you're going. The road remains one way for about 4.2 more miles, to the Park boundary. Then be alert; traffic may come from the opposite direction. Follow this winding road down the mountain about 2.7 miles to a three-way intersection. Bearing to the right, take the middle road. Continue 1.1 miles to intersection with Tuckaleechee Caverns road. Keep left. Continue .7 of a mile to a cemetery at a cross road. Turn left and follow this paved road about 1.3 miles to State Highway 73.

If you make the drive in July, look for the tall pink phlox along the mountain road.

16 BRADLEY FORK and HUGHES RIDGE
18 miles, round trip
See No. 16 on map

Eat an early breakfast. A big one. If you have to count calories this hike isn't for you, anyway. While hiking 18 miles, you also climb—and then descend—nearly 3000 feet, from 2198 feet above sea level at the Smokemont Campground starting and ending point to 5170 at the highest point on Hughes Ridge.

I made this loop hike September 7, supposedly a drab time outdoors. Most of the birds glide songlessly. Most fall flowers are yet to bloom. Autumn colors are only starting. Nevertheless, this was a rewarding jaunt.

Going up the Jeep road by Bradley Fork, I found hearts-a-bustin-with-love (Euonymus americanus) opening red-pink shells to expose orange-red seeds. Blue lobelia bloomed beautifully. Touch-me-nots were plentiful. Joe Pye weeds eight feet tall were purple-topped with bloom. A few sourwood leaves had turned bright blood red.

I picked Concord grapes in a clearing, probably an old home site.

Yellowing leaves of wild iris, red berries of false Solomon's seal and Jack-in-the-pulpit, patches of violets and hepaticas were proof this is a good spring wildflower trail. A large patch of pink lady's slippers grows in a little flat to the right of the trail. They'll bloom in May and June.

To the left of the road ran the stream. Trout held against the current and waited for it to bring brunch.

Tulip poplars, maples, buckeyes, dogwoods, sourwoods and basswoods grow in the valley. Basswoods send up many sprouts from old stumps. I counted more than 25, some 18 inches thick, growing from where two old stumps had stood close together.

After five miles of good grade along the creek, you reach a trail forks. Tired? Then here's the place to start back the route you came. But turn right if you want to continue. This is the Taywa Creek Trail. You'll soon see Taywa Creek bouncing along to your right.

I rounded a curve and saw a bear eating something on the road bank. He saw me, wheeled and ran up the road as fast as he could, his paws flapping and scratching the ground. Then he left the road and ran up into the woods. This was a wild bear. Not a tourist-fed panhandler. He did what most wild bears will do under similar circumstances —ran uphill.

I failed to discover what he had been eating. But I did find trailing arbutus on the bank. This was the first of a great deal of it on this trail. The air along the trail will be filled with its aroma when it blooms in April and May, or maybe earlier.

Soon I saw another bear. She was a dozen feet up a tree 40 yards away, eating something in the foliage. She saw me and backed down the trunk. Three cubs raced into view and went away with her.

I found twisted stalk, with ruby berries hanging where bell-shaped, rose-colored flowers had hung in May or June. Another springtime beauty growing here is painted trillium.

Suddenly, in this "birdless" season, there was a congregation of birds—at least three kinds of warblers, golden-crowned kinglets, brown creepers and a woodpecker. But I doubt the woodpecker was "with" the others.

Within one-fourth mile of the ridge top, I found a rarity—native chestnut sprouts large enough to bear. One sprout was about a foot in diameter, another a little larger. Burrs littered the ground. But the chestnuts were poor, shriveled things. Maybe the season had been too dry. Or perhaps the blight which was working on the trunks had cut short the nutrition the nuts needed.

Only yards from where the Taywa Creek Road intersects the Hughes Ridge Road at the ridge crest, orange-red hobble bush leaves made the prettiest color splash of the trip.

From here, you have 10 miles to go, along the winding trail that follows the ridge crest much of the way back to camp. It is mostly down hill. The trail is soft, more pleasant than the Jeep road was.

The first four or five miles wind through a wonderful dry-type forest. Acres of mountain tea, trailing arbutus and galax cover the ground. Mountain laurel and rhododendron grow thickly.

Till now, water has been plentiful—from Bradley Fork and Taywa Creek. But there are no springs during dry weather on the first half or two-thirds of the Hughes Ridge Trail. But you probably can make it without a canteen until you start finding springs along the last few miles.

I picked and ate blueberries along the ridge top.

17 ANDREWS BALD
4 miles, round trip
See No. 17 on map

This hike is good for nearly any time, except when snow lies too deeply on the trail.

Try it on a day in May when spring is opening the first wild flowers in this mile-high-plus area.

Sometime after the middle of June, flame azalea and rose-purple rhododendron bloom on the bald.

If you like blueberries, September is the time to go to Andrews.

Go in October and look at the gold and purple hills in the far distance.

If you're in the proper mood, it can be unusually rewarding to walk through the green gloom of the spruce-fir forest

on a rainy day when all is silent except for the soft fall of the rain and the gentle moan of the wind.

It is an easy hike. Starting point is the Clingmans Dome parking area. The first part of the trail is the least pleasant. It is steepest and rockiest and it runs through an area of ragged growth that isn't particularly attractive. This is because it was swept by fire in the middle 1920s. However, it's good territory for birders. The winter wren, veery, Carolina junco and some of the warblers are nearly always present in spring and summer.

Within a half-mile, you'll be out of the burned-over area and into virgin spruce-fir forest. Here is a view of nature at work, unaided and unimpeded by man. Walk a few yards off the trail and look at the great tangle of fallen tree trunks, some down only a few months and others for many decades. They're in various stages of decay. New growth feeds upon them. This is the unhurried cycle of growth, death, decay and growth again.

Notice the little wood sorrel (Oxalis montana) growing thickly in the dark-lace shade in the thick spruce-fir stands. A plant far less pretty growing along this trail is commonly called mountain ragweed. Just before you reach the bald, if you make the trip around the midde of June, you may find tiny wild lilies of the valley.

Like nearly all the grass balds of the Great Smokies, Andrews has some heath plants. Those you'll be most interested in, if you make the trip during the second half of June—say around June 15-25—are Catawba (rose-purple) rhododendron and flame azalea. The rhododendron grows on the higher part of the bald, the portion you reach first. To see the best azaleas—and to find water—you must walk on down the slope to the southern edge of the bald.

Go in late August or the first half of September for blueberries. They usually ripen over a period of nearly a month. To be certain of the best time to find them in a given season, consult a naturalist at the Sugarlands Visitor Center, near Park Headquarters, at Gatlinburg. These are high-bush blueberries. Some of the bushes grow far higher than your head.

Arriving when berries are ripe is no guarantee of finding many berries. Bears may have harvested them. They gorge on them.

At 5680 feet above sea level, Andrews is the highest grass bald in the Park. Most of the other well-known balds in the Park—Gregory Bald, Silers Bald and Spence Field— are on the main crest of the Great Smokies, divided between Tennessee and North Carolina. But Andrews is entirely within Carolina.

Of the major grass balds it is the easiest for the hiker to reach. It also offers the best azalea show for small effort in getting there. However, Andrews azaleas don't approach the big display on Gregory.

There are only two intersections on the trail and you take the left fork—on the way to the bald—both times. The first intersection is only a few hundred yards from the parking area. The right fork leads to the Appalachian Trail. The second intersection is near the middle point of the hike. The right fork here goes down to Forney Creek. Don't take it—unless you want to fish for native brook trout.

18 DEEP CREEK - INDIAN CREEK
4 miles, round trip
See No. 18 on map

This might be called the "Hearts-A-Bustin'-With-Love Hike" or the "Waterfall Hike."

If you do it in late summer or early autumn, you'll find hearts-a-bustin'-with-love (Euonymus americanus) displaying rose-pink shells and orange-red berries every few yards along the entire hike. This little wild shrub grows very well in this area. The National Park Service has planted several clumps of it in Deep Creek Campgroud.

The campground is about three miles north of Bryson City, N. C. Your trail starts a few yards north of it and

runs to the left of and parallel to Deep Creek. You'll see your first waterfall about 1000 feet beyond the trail start.

This is Toms Branch Falls. Lovely! An expert landscaper couldn't have done half as well as nature did. The small stream tumbles 60 or 70 feet into Deep Creek on the side of the creek opposite the trail. The fall is broken into a half-dozen rock-ledge levels. When the stream is low, the water switches from one side to the other between drops.

Your "trail" actually is a Jeep road for the first mile and a half. It switches back and forth across the creek a few times by way of wooden bridges.

Follow it a short mile, to the point where the road forks, the right fork going up Indian Creek and the left one up Deep Creek. I suggest you go left. But it doesn't much matter. For at this point you begin a loop. If you go left, though, you'll save Indian Creek Falls till near the end of the hike. If it's a hot day, you may want to get cool in the pool below the falls.

Notice the sand and rocks in the road. Those silvery particles are mica.

In springtime you'll see trillium, Solomon seal, false Solomon seal, dog hobble, violets, Jack-in-the-pulpit, dogwoods and other spring flowers in bloom along this trail. Some grow to giant size. I saw a Solomon seal six feet tall when pulled straight up from its normal bent posture. Dogwoods are particularly numerous along the Deep Creek leg of the loop.

Fall flowers here include many asters, golden rod, iron weed, blue lobelia and red lobelia or cardinal flower.

Watch for the marker for the trail onto which you turn right. It's only a dozen feet beyond a bridge over which you cross to the right of the creek.

Follow this trail one mile over Sunkata Ridge to the road that runs beside Indian Creek. The ridge trail has enough laurel and rhododendron for a fine show in years when bloom is good. Also, look along it for trailing arbutus and galax. You'll find pink lady's slippers just after you top the ridge and start down toward Indian Creek. They bloom in late May or early June.

This is second-growth timber, with pines and oaks predominating, along the ridge trail. Near the intersection of the ridge trail and Indian Creek Road is the stone foundation of a building, but the building is gone. This area once was inhabited. Indian Creek School stood somewhere in this vicinity, according to old maps.

Turn right on the road and follow it down Indian Creek to the falls, actually a pretty cascade which ends in a wide pool.

19 SHUCKSTACK - TWENTY MILE CREEK

Suggested route about 9.25 miles, round trip
See No. 19 on map

High school and college football players wanting legs and lungs at their best in September might try getting summer jobs in the Fontana Dam section. A daily hike up Shuckstack Mountain will remove surplus pounds, build leg power and multiply stamina.

But if you're a middle-aged adult with cardiac troubles, rest often when you climb Shuckstack. Or ride a horse. However, adults in good physical condition should experience no trouble with it.

Several years ago, Edward N. Little, then 65, of Englewood, N. J., and Murray S. Chism, Tenafly, N. J., only 18 months younger, hiked the entire Appalachian Trail from Georgia to Maine, each carrying a pack weighing more than 35 pounds. The climb up Shuckstack was only a fraction of their trip. The trail used then was steeper than the one used now. The 2300-foot altitude gain from Fontana Dam to the top of Shuckstack was made then over a 2.5-mile trail which mounted steep places the most direct way, climbing contour lines like stairsteps. The trail used now is much easier but about three-quarters of a mile longer.

The trail is excellent for wildflowers. On a day in late April I saw three species of trillium, three or four species of violets, including the lovely birdfoot violet; pink lady's-slipper; yellow lady's slipper, which is one of the rarest flowers of outstanding beauty in the Park; dogwood; silverbell and many less showy flowers.

Two or three weeks later, I could have seen mountain laurel blooming near the top of Shuckstack. It grows thickly along a narrow, rocky spine east of the fire tower atop Shuckstack. The old trail followed this spine.

Only 4020 feet above sea level, Shucktack is not as high as several other peaks in the Great Smokies. But it is positioned in a way to give outstanding views to those who climb it.

It isn't absolutely necessary to climb the fire tower, but the tower does gives a longer panoramic view. To the north lies the main range of the Great Smokies, visible for a stretch of some 30 miles—from west of Gregory Bald eastward to Clingmans Dome. On a clear day, the Gregory and Spence Field grass balds are easily distinguishable. So is the ragged western slope of Mt. Buckley, just west of Clingmans.

Turn to the southwest. Down there is Fontana Lake, lying like a green dragon between the mountains, stretching appendages up narrow tributary valleys. Look to the southwest, where a portion of Cheoah Lake can be seen.

Let your eyes rove the mountains south of the Little Tennessee River Valley, the ranges of the Cheoah and Snowbird Mountains. Southward, on a line a little to the east of Fontana Dam, is Wauchecha Bald, 4385 feet above sea level. It is one of the prominent Cheoah peaks.

If you're in a hurry, you can retrace your steps to the dam, for a 6.5-mile round trip. However, if you can arrange to have transportation waiting for you, you'll enjoy a 6.5-mile return to State Highway 28, where Twenty-Mile Creek pours into Cheoah Lake. This route is by jeep trail. The grade is much easier than you followed from the dam to the mountain top. The final three miles parallel the creek. The road passes the ranger station, which is only a few yards from the highway.

Twenty-Mile Creek gets its name from the fact that the distance is 20 miles from its mouth to the mouth of Hazel Creek. It's a good rainbow trout stream. Deep pools, cascades and falls also make it a delightfully pretty creek. Watch for a marker which will direct you to a particularly pretty cascade.

Some may prefer to do this hike in reverse—going up Shuckstack by way of the jeep road and descending the steep part to the dam.

Carry water if the day is a warm one. There's no drinking water along the way, except for the 3-mile stretch along the creek.

20 THE APPALACHIAN TRAIL
Nearly 70 miles, one way
See No. 20 on map

The nation's most famous footpath is the 2000-mile Appalachian Trail. The AT reaches its highest elevation, passes some of its loveliest scenes and rambles over some of its ruggedest territory in its 70-mile stretch in Great Smoky Mountains National Park.

Smoky Mountain Council of Boy Scouts of America gives a special Appalachian Trail Award to Scouts who hike the part of the AT in the Great Smokies.

For the long hiker who wants to spend an entire vacation along it, the AT offers some of the best wild scenic beauty in America, trailside shelters, interesting side hikes, things to see and streams to fish. Usually—but not always—one who wants it can find solitude along the long trail.

It also offers many possibilities for those wanting to make shorter hikes of a day or less. Many of these are mentioned in previous chapters.

One of the best features of the AT is that it offers a worthwhile challenge to young men who want to test their endurance, will and muscle. Several have run for the record along it. As far as I know, two young men from Karns community in West Knox County hold the record. These two—Max Kirtland and Earl Keller—hiked from Davenport Gap to Fontana Dam in 25 hours and 28 minutes, July 19-20, 1954. Max was 18 and Earl was 17. They averaged nearly 2.7 miles per hour.

Most hikers who set out to do the entire portion of the AT inside the Park start at Davenport Gap, which is at the eastern end of the Park, at the Tennessee-North Carolina line. The approaches to this point are State Highway 32 from Cosby, Tenn., and State 284 from the North Carolina side. The alternative is to start at Fontana Dam and hike northeastward to Davenport Gap. But it's easier the other way. Though the net drop in elevation from Davenport Gap (2000 feet) to the paved road at Fontana Dam (about 1727 feet) is less than 275 feet, this is not the major advantage. The advantage is that by going from northeast to southwest, one is able to descend—rather than climb—steep Mt. Buckley and Shuckstack Mountain.

Eighteen trailside shelters at 14 sites along the AT will keep rain and snow off nearly 200 persons. But they offer little protection from cold, since they are open on one side. Each site has a pit toilet and water supply. Each site has a stone shelter large enough for at least a dozen persons. Four sites also have older log shelters which accommodate six persons each.

Those getting on the trail late in the day may want to stop at the first shelter, only about nine-tenths of a mile west of Davenport Gap. It accommodates 12.

The first leg of this hike is described in Chapter 9 (Mt. Cammerer). Don't fail to take the short side trip to Mt. Cammerer Tower. Here is one of the finest panoramic views in the Great Smokies. Rhododendron and laurel bloom on Cammerer and are beautiful in late spring.

Between Cammerer and Low Gap, a little less than three miles to the west, are Sunup Knob and Rocky Face Mountain. Both offer moderately good views. (I once got an excellent view of a large wildcat near the top of Rocky Face. One advantage of hiking alone is that one sometimes comes upon wildcats or foxes before they hear you.)

A transmountain trail intersects the AT at Low Gap. To the north the trail runs 2.5 miles down to Cosby Campground. To the south, it goes 2.5 miles to Walnut Bottoms, on Big Creek, in North Carolina.

Approximately a mile west of Low Gap is Cosby Knob Shelter, accommodating 12. Between the gap and the shelter is a beautiful mixed forest of cherry and birch. Most of the trees are young, probably indicating that fire burned over the area about 40 years ago. The tiny cherries ripen in late August and early September. They're tart but tasty. Also between the gap and the shelter is a lovely spring. Its waters rise from the root area of a big birch to the right of the trail and run in silvery rivulets down a mossy bank.

West of the shelter, higher on Cosby Knob, is a wooly area that provides blueberries and blackberries to hungry hikers in August and September. Serviceberries ripen here in late June.

Going on west of Cosby Knob, one crosses such places as Ross Knob, Camel Gap, Camel Hump Knob, Inadu Knob and Yellow Creek Gap. It's up-and-down hiking in fairly open country. A hiker looking southward gets occasional marvelous views of Big Creek Valley, Luftee Knob, Big

Cataloochee Knob and Mt. Sterling. Portions of the trail in this area are extremely rocky.

Farther west loom the challenging heights of Old Black and Mt. Guyot. At 6621 feet, Guyot is the second highest point in the Great Smokies. The AT doesn't cross Guyot's summit. But an old manway, clogged and often hidden by blown-down trees, meanders three-quarters of a mile to the domed top. This least accessible of the major Great Smokies peaks is visited far less frequently than Clingmans Dome and Mt. Le Conte. It is covered with spruce and fir— mostly fir—and offers no spectacular view. The major satisfaction in reaching the top of Guyot is the knowledge that you've just become a member of a pretty exclusive club. The manway isn't easy to follow. Some thoughtful club member once blazed a few trees along it, and a later one tacked up markers of persimmon-colored plastic.

Back on the AT, a few yards west of the manway, is Guyot Spring. Rising on the shaded north slope about 6300 feet above sea level, the spring water is very cold. It is the top headwater of Ramsey Prong. This cold water gets a wild and lovely ride down over Ramsey Cascades.

Tri-Corner Knob is less than two miles west of the spring. This is where Balsam Mountain ties onto the main crest of the Great Smokies. The Balsam Mountain Trail breaks off the AT here and runs southeasterly along the Balsam crest. A little west of the summit are the Tri-Corner shelters—one accommodating 12 and the other six persons.

The first major peak west of Tri-Corner is Mt. Chapman, named for David Chapman, one of the leaders in the campaign to establish the national park in the Great Smokies. The trail swings south of the 6417-foot Chapman summit. On both sides of the trail west of the summit, rose-purple rhododendron grows thickly in otherwise sparse forest. It usually provides a good flower show in late June.

West of Mt. Chapman is Mt. Sequoyah, which the trail crosses at 6003 feet. It is unspectacular, and so is Copper Gap, next named place westward. But then comes Eagle Rocks Mountain. And in this vicinity, at the right edge of the trail, is a large rock in which is imbedded a bench mark which gives the elevation as 5849 feet. Standing atop the rock, one looks nearly straight down into the extremely rugged valley of Eagle Rocks Prong and on down into the valley of Middle Prong of the Little Pigeon and Greenbrier Cove and across at Greenbrier Pinnacle.

Next westward is Pecks Corner. This is where Hughes Ridge, coming in from the North Carolina side, joins the main range. The Hughes Ridge Trail connects with the AT here, and nearly a half-mile down this trail is the 12-man Pecks Corner Shelter. It is 5.8 miles west of the Tricorner Knob Shelter and 3.2 miles east of the next shelter, at False Gap.

Between Pecks Corner and False Gap is Laurel Top, offering good views of Bradley Fork Valley, N. C.

The False Gap Shelter, several hundred feet north of the trail, sleeps 12.

Going on westward, one crosses Porters Mountain (5572 feet), dips into Porters Gap (5400 feet) and then ascends slightly to The Sawteeth, the jagged, raggedy range between Porters Gap and Dry Sluice Gap. There are good views from The Sawteeth, but not as good as from Charlies Bunion, just ahead. (See Hike No. 12 for description of the Bunion and the area westward to Newfound Gap.) About a mile west of the Bunion are the Ice Water Springs Shelters, sleeping a total of 18.

The 7.5 trail miles from Newfound Gap to Clingmans Dome parallel the automobile spur road to the Forney Ridge Parking Area, near the Dome. While most of the highway is hidden from the trail, hikers nearly always can hear cars. For many, this dulls some of the pleasure of the hike. But it is a good stretch of trail, in spite of the cars.

Indian Gap, over which passed one of the Great Smokies' earliest roads, is a little less than two miles west of Newfound Gap. Running down the Tennessee side from the Gap is the Old Indian Road Trail, one of the loveliest in the mountains. (See No. 1 hike.) About 3.5 miles west of Newfound Gap is the intersection with the Sugarland Mountain Trail. On this trail, about a half-mile north of the AT, is the Mt. Collins Shelter for 12.

Then comes Collins Gap, after which one starts the climb to Mt. Love (6366 feet), sort of an eastern shoulder of Clingmans Dome. This is beautiful Great Smokies high country. Spruce and fir trees grow thickly from the mucky humus of their fallen forefathers. The ground usually is damp. Pink turtlehead flowers grow here. Moss, ferns and wood sorrel, sometimes called mountain shamrock, carpet the ground.

Between Mt. Love and Clingmans is a little gap. Then comes the ascent to the great Dome, 6643 feet above sea level, the highest point in the Great Smokies. On top of it is a 45-foot observation tower. A large wild blackberry patch is not far east of the Dome. The fruit usually doesn't ripen before late September, and freezing weather sometimes comes before it ripens.

Less than a half-mile west of Clingmans Dome is Mt. Buckley (6582 feet), the Dome's western shoulder. It is a raggedy, magnificent mountain, sort of a bald in need of a haircut. The view from up here sometimes is wonderful around the middle of June. On the Tennessee side, the jumbled mountains are marked with dozens of laurel slicks roan with rhododendron bloom. A cool wind nearly always blows across the narrow mountain crest.

About 3.25 miles west of the Dome is Double Springs Gap, site of a 12-man shelter. Two miles farther west are two more shelters, sleeping a total of 18, at Silers Bald.

(For a fuller account of the Clingmans Dome-Silers section, see Hike No. 11.)

At the eastern base of Silers, the trail forks, the left fork going down Welch Ridge and the right one (the AT) up over Silers through a grove of stunted beech trees. Fishermen may want to take the Welch Ridge Trail and branch off it onto an old abandoned manway that goes to Hazel Creek.

The AT is relatively little used from Silers westward to Thunderhead Mountain, about 11 rugged miles. One descends rather sharply to Buckeye Gap, then comes Cold Springs Knob, then an unnamed gap, Hemlock Knob, another unnamed gap, Mt. Davis, Sams Gap and Derrick Knob. A shelter at Derrick Knob, about 5.75 miles west of the Silers Bald Shelters, accommodates 12.

If in doubt about whether to spend the night at the Derrick Knob Shelter or to go on to the next shelters 5.5 miles westward at Spence Field, consider this: The trail between the two points probably is the ruggedest stretch of AT in the Great Smokies. It goes up and down from gap to knob. First is Sugar Tree Gap, followed by an unnamed knob, Starkey Gap, Brier Knob (a real lung buster), Mineral Gap, unnamed knob, Beechnut Gap, unnamed knob, unnamed gap, and then the climb up Thunderhead (5527 feet), then an unnamed gap, Rocky Top, and then another one or two ups and downs before one comes to the trail leading left to the old six-man shelter.

The view from Thunderhead is the best since Mt. Cammerer. Here is a place to rest and look and look.

Beyond the trail to the old shelter is a trail to the right which leads to Cades Cove and one to the left which leads to the new 12-man shelter and to the Eagle Creek Trail and trout fishing.

(For a fuller account of Spence Field and Thunderhead, see Hike No. 4.)

Westward from Spence Field the AT winds through sparse forest which, in late April and early May, is carpeted with a great variety of wildflowers. Chief species are spring beauties, adder's-tongue, trillium and many violets. Then one reaches a beautiful small clearing, Mt. Squires, once known as Little Bald, where there is a good view into North Carolina.

Next point of interest is Russell Field, where there is a 12-man shelter, (2.9 miles west of Spence Field), and an interesting one-time grassy bald which is now becoming wooly with invading trees and shrubs. Down the valley on the Tennessee side grow hundreds of serviceberry trees. This probably is the most outstanding serviceberry orchard in the Great Smokies. The bloom is lovely in late April. Berries usually ripen in June or early July. Trail to right leads to Anthony Creek Trail and Cades Cove Campground.

Along the next 4.5 miles of the AT one passes such places as Big Abrams Gap (Mill Creek, an Abrams Creek tributary, rises just below it on the Tennessee side), the Devil's Tater Patch (4752 feet), the Mollies Ridge Shelter (2.2 miles from Russell Field Shelter, sleeps 12.) Ekaneetlee Gap (across which ran an old transmountain trail linking Tennessee and North Carolina), Powell Knob, Mud Gap and Doe Knob.

This stretch is not spectacular. But it is pleasant if one has time to pause and enjoy occasional flame azalea blooms and other sights typical of a mountain hardwood forest.

The AT changes abruptly at Doe Knob, breaking off the crest of the Great Smokies and swinging southward. It formerly followed the main crest about 9.5 miles farther, crossing Gregory Bald and Parson Bald and leaving the Park at Deals Gap, at U. S. Highway 129. Now that it breaks off the crest at Doe Knob, the AT leaves the Park at Fontana Dam, about six miles from Doe Knob.

This six-mile stretch is a good reason for hiking the AT from east to west. The descent from Doe Knob is steep. After reaching a low point, one climbs gradually around Greer Knob without actually crossing its summit.

Birch Springs Shelter, which sleeps 12, is 2.2 miles from Doe Knob and about 4.5 miles from the Mollies Ridge

Shelter. The shelter is about 100 yards to the right of the trail.

Sassafras Gap is the next point of interest. One leaves the AT here for a half-mile climb to the Shuckstack Lookout. It's worth it. (Jeep road runs from this point about six miles down to Twenty Mile Creek Valley and on down to North Carolina Highway 28). But, to continue on the AT, follow trail to left down to the dam.

(For detailed account of Shuckstack-to-dam hike, see Hike No. 19.)

Boy Scouts may earn an Appalachian Trail Award by hiking the portion of the AT inside the Park in not more than four trips. I'd suggest it be done in one, two or four trips.

If you do it in one trip, make it a five-day jaunt with these daily distances: Davenport Gap to Tricorner Knob, nearly 16 miles, first day; Tricorner to Ice Water Springs, a little more than 12 miles, second day; Ice Water Springs to Silers Bald, about 15 miles, third day; Silers to Spence Field, about 11.5 miles, fourth day; Spence Field to Fontana, nearly 14 miles, fifth day. This gives one an overnight stop at places with two shelters with accommodations for 18 each night on the trail.

For those doing it in two trips, I suggest starting each trip at Newfound Gap. For one two-day hike, go eastward from Newfound and spend the night at Tricorner Knob and go on to Davenport Gap the next day. You'll hike about 15 miles the first day and 16 the second. For the second trip, go westward from Newfound to Silers Bald, about 12 miles, the first day, from Silers to Spence Field the second day and from Spence to Fontana the third.

Those doing the AT in four separate trips might try it this way:

First day, go from Newfound Gap eastward to Tricorner Knob. And go the next day from Tricorner to Low Gap and from Low Gap to Cosby Campground, nearly 11 miles. The next trip is a one-day one, from Cosby Campground up to Low Gap and then eastward on the AT to Davenport Gap, a hike of about 9.25 miles. The third trip is from Newfound Gap westward to Silers Bald, nearly 12 miles, the first day, and from Silers to Spence Field and then down the Bote Mountain-Anthony Creek Trails to Cades Cove Campground, 16 or 17 miles, the second day. The fourth trip is from Cades Cove Campground to Spence Field and then westward on the AT to Russell Field, about

12.6 miles, the first day, and from Russell Field to Fontana Dam, about 11.25 miles, the second day.

Besides the hikes, requirements for the Award include: (1) getting approval of your unit leader before starting on any of them, (2) writing a brief account of hikes, giving dates, points of departure and destination, companions, camping permit serial numbers and things of interest on the trip, (3) writing summaries of the histories of the AT and Great Smoky Mountains National Park, showing that you are aware of the efforts of those who worked to preserve the beauties of the mountains and to make possible the 2000-mile AT, and (4) submit accounts of your trips, with leader's approval, to Great Smoky Mountain Council, Boy Scouts of America, Knoxville, Tenn.

You'll receive an attractive patch and a great deal of fun and satisfaction for your efforts.

21 SUGARLAND MOUNTAIN
Slightly more than 13 miles, one way
See 21 on map

A brief burst of noise ripped a hole in the gentle sound of rain on the forest leaves. A ruffed grouse made it when he exploded upward from the ground to a perch on a small dead pine beside the trail.

He was startled and puzzled. He had heard the raspy rustle of my rain suit as I walked down the trail, but he hadn't seen me. His back was to me. But his head was darting nervously to right and left. He was about 15 yards ahead of me. I had a close-up look at him for nearly a minute. Then he saw me. There was a longer explosion of sound, and he was gone.

This was on an April morning, on a hike down the Sugarland Mountain Trail. The starting point was the Spruce-Fir Nature Trail on the Clingmans Dome Road. The nature trail intersects the Appalachian Trail at the point where the Sugarland Trail joins the AT. From that point down to the end of the hike on Tennessee Highway 73, at Fighting Creek Gap, is about 13 miles. The altitude range is from a little more than 6000 feet at a point on the nature trail, near the top of Mt. Collins, to about 2240 feet at Tennessee 73. But it isn't all down-hill walking. The trail dips into gaps and then climbs again to high points.

My wife drove me to the starting point of the hike and was waiting to pick me up at the end of it four hours later.

April is an interesting time to make this hike, for winter usually still rules the mountaintop in April, but one walks down into spring. Spring beauties and yellow violets were the first bits of spring color I saw. Farther down the trail, five or six miles from the starting point, were masses of trailing arbutus, just beginning to bloom. Still farther down the mountain were white trillium, Dutchman's breeches and bloodroot, all in bloom.

And I saw a patch or two of ramps. The ramp (Allium tricoccum) is a member of the lily family. It was the first green thing fit to eat that pioneer mountaineers could gather in the early spring. Of course, there is debate over whether ramps are fit to eat. Though the new green leaves are tender and not particularly bad to the taste, the odor lingers long on the breath of the eater. Some mountain people, as well as a few East Tennessee and Western North Carolina city dwellers still eat ramps.

Sugarland Mountain is the high divide separating Little River Valley, on the west, from the valley of West Fork of the Little Pigeon, to the east. About a third of the way down the trail, one can look down to the right at the Chimney Tops, the spectacular twin peaks on Sugarland's northeastern flank.

Masses of laurel grow here and there along the trail below the 5000-foot elevation, making this a good hike for May and June. Generally, the higher the elevation the later the bloom.

22 COOPER ROAD - GOLD MINE ROAD
About 9 miles
See 22 on map

This is an excellent early-spring hike, when trailing arbutus blooms. Cooper Road crosses Arbutus Ridge, aptly named for the little trailing plants with leathery leaves and sweet-smelling flowers that grow on it in unusual abundance. Pink lady's slippers also are numerous. They bloom a little later. Cardinal flowers grow near the small streams and brighten this hike in early autumn.

Oldtimers say this was the first road from Cades Cove to Maryville. Pioneer Cove dwellers traveled it on foot, by horseback and in wagons and buggies. It was a two-day drive with a herd of cattle to market in Maryville.

Miners found gold in small quantities near what is now the western boundary of the Park. Thus, the name of the old road on the western end of the hike.

To start at the eastern end of the hike, drive the Cades Cove Loop Road 4.2 miles from its beginning to where old road (the one you will hike) starts off right side of Loop Road. First trail intersection, 5.5 miles from starting point, is with Abrams Falls-Beard Cane Mountain Trail. Next intersection is where Beard Cane Branch Trail branches right. Next is Cooper Road-Gold Mine Road intersection. Continue right on Gold Mine Road one mile to Park boundary.

To start hike at western end, leave Foothills Parkway at Look Rock and drive 2.2 miles down road into Top O' The World development. This brings you to an old unimproved road which leads to your right down to the park boundary. Park car at first convenient place on the old road, for it is too rough for most vehicles except Jeeps. This is Gold Mine Road. Follow it one mile to where it joins Cooper Road and continue left on Cooper.

Most persons will find this hike too long as a round-tripper. So you should arrange to have a car waiting at the end of a one-way hike.

60

23
SCOTT GAP, CADES COVE
About 12.5 miles
See 23 on map

This trail might be called the Huckleberry Trail in late July or early August, when those small, sweet fruits are ripening. Huckleberry bushes grow thickly on Hannah Mountain, where first seven miles of this hike wind through pleasant woodland. Wild iris, rue anemone, goat's beard are among flowers along trail.

Trail intersects the old Rabbit Creek Road at Scott Gap. Turn right on it and follow it eastward to Abrams Creek Parking Area, where Mill Creek runs into Abrams.

Starting point of hike is Sams Gap, on the Parson Branch Road, about three miles from the entrance gate on this one-way road. Parson Branch Road is open only during summer and parts of spring and fall months. And gates are closed at night. So any car left at starting point should be recovered before darkness.

24
BUNKER HILL TOWER
About 5 miles, round trip
See 24 on map

This is a fairly easy trail, as Great Smokies trails go, through a forest of mostly pines and oaks. Galax, trailing arbutus and teaberry are among interesting small flowering plants. By climbing tower one can get excellent view of the southwestern end of the park. Starting point of hike is about 4.5 miles south of the gate of the one-way Parson Branch Road, which is open only during summer and part of spring and fall months.

Net altitude gain is about 220 feet.

25

SINKS TO JAKES CREEK
About 10 miles, one way
See 25 on map

This hike starts at the parking area at the Sinks, that spectacular pool in Little River, beside State Highway 73, between Townsend and Gatlinburg. Trail climbs first over a western lead of Curry He Mountain and then dips down into Meigs Creek Valley and follows this delightful little stream for a mile or more. Fine forest of large trees, many of them hemlocks, grows here. Look for a lovely, large beech tree to left of trail.

Trail leaves valley and climbs to Buckhorn Gap, where it is joined by an old trail from right. (Old trail goes down into valley of Little River's Middle Prong.) Continue left to Upper Buckhorn Gap, looking along the way for a grouse wallow. It's a circular depression about a yard in diameter and close to a foot deep, right on the trail. Another dim old trail joins from right at Upper Buckhorn. Continue left. Next intersecting trail goes to Metcalf Bottoms. Continue right. From this point, look for old stone fences and other indications that area once was farmed.

You're near the end of the hike when you have to cross a fence into Lem Ownby's cow pasture. At this writing, Mr. Ownby's about 80, and he's lived all his life at or near this same place. He holds a life lease on a small parcel of property inside park. From his house, follow trail across Jakes Creek to Jakes Creek truck road and down to Elkmont, where you should have transportation waiting.

26

CUCUMBER GAP TRAIL
5 miles, round trip
See 26 on map

This is one of the most delightful short hikes in the Great Smokies. Wildflowers bloom along it in great numbers in spring. It has no high hills. It connects Little River, on the east, with Jakes Creek, on the west.

Starting point from Little River is 3.1 miles up Little River Road from Elkmont Campground entrance. Starting point from Jakes Creek is gate beyond which cars may not go on Jakes Creek Road. Walk about a half-mile up road to where your trail starts from left side of road.

27

LITTLE RIVER - HUSKEY GAP
Nearly four miles, round trip
See 27 on map

This is another good short hike, similar in some respects to No. 26. But the grade on this is steeper. Much mountain laurel blooms along it near Huskey Gap.

Upon reaching the gap, one can turn back to the starting point. But if the hikers have more than one car, they have other choices. They can turn north at the gap and follow the Sugarland Mountain Trail three miles to Fighting Creek Gap, on State Highway 73. Or they can continue eastward two miles to U.S. Highway 441. Those with lots of ambition may want to turn southward at the gap and follow the Sugarland Mountain Trail to the top of the mountain at Mt. Collins. (See Hike No. 18.)

28

U.S. 441 to HUSKEY GAP
About 4 miles, round trip
See 28 on map

This is another good short hike. Starting point is from west side of U.S. Highway 441, 1.7 miles south of intersection of 441 and State 73, at Park Visitor Center.

It's good for wildflowers in spring and autumn colors in fall. One spot on trail, near Huskey Gap, offers a fine view of Mt. LeConte, across West Prong Valley, to the east.

Once at the gap, one can go back to starting point, go on westward to Little River, or go up or down Sugarland Mountain Trail. (See No. 18.)

29

DRIPPING SPRINGS MOUNTAIN - MIRY RIDGE
17 miles, round trip
See 29 on map

Starting point of this hike is same as that for No. 13, to Blanket Mountain, and the route is the same the four miles to Jakes Gap. But take trail to left at that point, which leads to Appalachian Trail, on the mountain crest, about 4.5 miles distant.

This is one of the most remote sections of the Park. Dripping Springs Mountain is well named. One can use a cup or cupped hands to drink from many of the drips.

A large heath bald, sporting the shining green of mountain laurel and rhododendron and the smaller heath plants like teaberry, galax and three varieties of club moss, is a good place to stop to do some looking on Miry Ridge. Miry Ridge also has a stand of red spruce, the westernmost spruce in the Park.

The trail intersects the Appalachian Trail a short distance west of Buckeye Gap and a short distance east of Cold Spring Knob.

30 MADDRON BALD
About 5 miles one way, 8 another way.
See 30 on map

Maddron Bald is a big heath bald, a giant hump sticking out on the north slope of the Great Smokies. Such shrubs as laurel, rhododendron, blueberry bushes and mountain myrtle grow here.

Shortest way to it is by way of the Snake Den Trail, out of Cosby Campground. It's five miles of steady climbing to the bald and a' half-mile more to the Appalachian Trail, on the crest of the Smokies, just east of Inadu Knob.

Those wanting an alternate route down, provided they can arrange a second car at the end, can go down the Indian Camp Creek Trail. It's an 8-mile jaunt. The lower portion of it, in the creek valley, has some of the park's finest woodland. The Albright Grove Nature Trail loops off this trail. On it grow some huge trees, including a tulip poplar believed to be the largest tree in the park. Those wanting to start this trail from the lower end should drive about 16.3 miles eastward on Tennessee 73 from intersection of 73 and U.S. 441, near Mountain View Hotel. A narrow road runs southward from 53, leaving 73 about .4 of a mile east of Sevier-Cocke County line. Follow old road .2 of a mile to where trail starts on right side of road.

31 SWEAT HEIFER TRAIL
About 7.5 miles, one way
See 31 on map

Starting at Newfound Gap, go east a mile and a half on the Appalachian Trail to the point where the Sweat Heifer Trail branches southward down the mountain. Nearly all of the rest of the hike is down hill.

It's a pleasant, little-used foot trail for the first approximately four miles down from the crest. Very easy on the feet. Then it runs into an old road, not so easy on the feet, for the final two miles to U.S. 441, close to where Kephart Prong runs into Oconaluftee River.